PRAISE FOR *THE OPENING PLAYBOOK*

So many experts have the sales formula wrong, always chasing the next transaction. When you are ready to transform your good relationships into lifelong brand lovers, read *The Opening Playbook*.

—Bolivar J. Bueno, founder, The Cult Branding Company,
and author, *Customers First*

In today's world of "do more with less," relationships are often sacrificed on the altar of transaction. Andrew Dietz shows how to lead with service and relationship in order to achieve your goals and to help your clients achieve theirs.

—Todd Henry, author, *Die Empty* and *The Accidental Creative*

I've read dozens of books before that cover all aspects of "selling," including prospecting, qualifying leads, networking, presenting, and closing. I never have read a book before that so simply and practically covers all of them in a way that anyone from a neophyte to journeyman sales professional can understand and immediately apply. Andrew cleverly utilizes sports analogies and playbooks to help drive key points home and show how any professional willing to study Andrew's playbook can make the business development All Star team.

—Bob Littell, author, *The Heart and Art of NetWeaving*

Professionals across myriad professional service businesses will benefit from cracking open Andrew Dietz's *The Opening Playbook*. Weaving real-world commentary into a fictional account of one aspiring professional's journey to success, Dietz outlines both the behavioral pitfalls to avoid and the disciplines to embrace on one's path to truly connecting with clients. Don't look for any phony sales tricks or manipulative marketing techniques here, no, no, no . . . only truly honest instruction from the Lombardi of business development coaches.

—James H. Gilmore, coauthor, *The Experience
Economy* and *Authenticity*

Andrew Dietz is a master at building relationships, and his book is filled with insightful ideas and useful strategies.

—Alan Deutschman, author, *Walk the Walk*
and *Change or Die*

The Opening Playbook should be subtitled *Moneyball for Business Development.* Dietz is a double-threat author, not only drawing up a superb game plan for hitting paydirt in business development, but making *The Opening Playbook* a damned entertaining read.

> —John Helyar, coauthor, business book bestseller
> *Barbarians at the Gate,* and author, *Lords of the Realm:*
> *The Real History of Baseball*

Andrew Dietz inspires you to create great conversations with your prospects so that you become a valuable, trusted advisor. He shows the best way to develop business by creating meaningful conversations. If you want long-term relationships with your clients, this is the book for you.

> —Shawn Kent Hayashi, author, *Conversations that*
> *Get Results and Inspire Collaboration*

In *The Opening Playbook,* Dietz provides a great blend of strategic and tactical advice, wrapped in great stories and examples. It's an enjoyable and *valuable* read!

> —Bill Cates, author, *Get More Referrals Now* and
> *Beyond Referrals*

If you want to have your clients for life, you must read *The Opening Playbook*! A great storyteller, Andrew Dietz provides invaluable insights on how to become a trusted advisor.

> —Jagdish N. Sheth, Charles H. Kellstadt Professor
> of Marketing, Emory University, and author,
> *Clients for Life*

THE
OPENING
PLAYBOOK

A Professional's Guide
to Building Relationships
that Grow Revenue

ANDREW DIETZ

New York Chicago San Francisco Athens London Madrid
Mexico City Milan New Delhi Singapore Sydney Toronto

1 2 3 4 5 6 7 8 9 0   DOC/DOC   1 2 0 9 8 7 6 5 4

ISBN   978-0-07-182588-7
MHID 0-07-182588-6

e-ISBN   978-0-07-182589-4
e-MHID 0-07-182589-4

Library of Congress Cataloging-in-Publication Data
Dietz, Andrew.
   The opening playbook : a professional's guide to building relationships that grow revenue / by Andrew Dietz.
      pages cm
   ISBN 978-0-07-182588-7 (alk. paper) — ISBN 0-07-182588-6 (alk. paper)
1. Business referrals. 2. Customer relations. I. Title.
   HF5438.25.D538 2014
   658.8—dc23

                                                                      2014002540

McGraw-Hill Education books are available at special quantity discounts to use as premiums and sales promotions or for use in corporate training programs. To contact a representative, please visit the Contact Us pages at www.mhprofessional.com.

For my wonderful, openhearted family.

CONTENTS

ACKNOWLEDGMENTS   ix

INTRODUCTION:
WIN THE COIN TOSS   xi

SECTION 1

Opening Plays

1   Don't Fumble the Kickoff   3

2   Establish Field Position   13

3   Nail the Opening Series   21

4   Establish Quarterback-Receiver Rhythm   29

5   Develop Pocket Presence   33

6   The Right Play at the Right Time   41

SECTION 2

Opening Strategy

7   Avoid the Scrum   47

8   Own the Open Field   57

SECTION 3

Right Connections:
The Relationship Advantage

9   The Triple Option Play   77

10   Plan Your Draft Picks   85

11   Respect Your Front Line   97

12   Be a Better Teammate   103

13   Find Open Receivers Fast   109

14   Master the Locker Room Speech   115

SECTION 4

**Right Conversations:
The Information Advantage**

15   Run, Pass, Kick   125

16   Call the Right Play   139

17   Command the Huddle   147

18   No Trick Plays   159

SECTION 5

**Right Context:
The Experience Advantage**

19   Show Your Skills   167

20   Your Prospects Aren't the Opposing Defense   171

21   Set the Tone for the Team   179

22   Play the Odds   183

23   Get More First Downs   189

SECTION 6

Open-Ended

24   Stay Open   197

25   Winning in the Red Zone   199

26   Coda and Resources   203

INDEX   211

ACKNOWLEDGMENTS

Many thanks to my colleagues, clients, and friends at Creative Growth Group, Inc., and CGG Alliance LLC for their ongoing input and support. Special thanks to Jay Busbee, without whose editorial support and friendship this book wouldn't have seen the light of day. And also to Gregg Bauer and his team at Bauerhaus Creative for their design contributions. Thanks, too, to a cadre of superb business writers and thinkers whom I'm lucky to know and who shared encouragement and counsel on this project: John Helyar, Jim Gilmore, Todd Henry, Alan Deutschman, Dr. Jagdish Sheth, and many others. I am extremely grateful, too, for the publishing confidence and editorial assistance provided by my key contacts at McGraw-Hill Education: Donya Dickerson, Dannalie Diaz, Pattie Amoroso, Eric Lowenkron, and Mary Glenn. And, of course, to Janice, Samantha, and Jessie, who are my ongoing opening inspiration.

INTRODUCTION: WIN THE COIN TOSS

Let's open with some "closing" words:

Closing is finite.

Closing is an end.

It's likely that you've been taught differently when the subject is sales. Our business culture promotes closing as the most vital element of selling. And why not? Closing implies tangible results *now*, not later.

In *The Opening Playbook*, we'll take a counterintuitive approach. Closing before you've appropriately opened a business relationship is the sound of a door shutting in your face.

Here's the mantra for the twenty-first century:
Always Be Opening.

Especially for professional services providers, opening a relationship the right way and keeping it open for the long run leads clients to step forward and to select you and your firm . . . and even to work with you again and again. Getting bought is better than selling. Also, the benefits of opening an authentic advisory relationship (a real relationship, not a manipulative one) accrue over time in a way the short-term, transactional drive to close deals never can.

Coaches, teams, and athletes rely on playbooks to define orchestrated plays, patterns, and progressions that increase the likelihood of scoring. In baseball, the more at bats you get, the more likely you are to score. Managers have defined strategies for making that happen. In football, the more often a team can get the ball in the red zone, the area within 20 yards of the opponent's goal line, the more likely it is to put points on the board. Football playbooks have frameworks for making that happen. In soccer, the third of the field where one team is trying to score against the opposing team is called the final third. Soccer playbooks have frameworks for getting players into that favorable position. In the same way, the business development framework in *The Opening Playbook* was crafted to more frequently put professionals in a position to be bought by their preferred prospects and clients of choice.

Technique and *finesse* are the operative words here. Once most professionals get in the room with an ideal prospect who has a real and immediate need for help, those professionals usually can do a fine job of demonstrating their differences and winning work. That's a play with a high probability of success. The problem is that too many professionals don't know how to get into that room in the first place. *The Opening Playbook* describes the best sequence of actions to put you, the soon to be trusted advisor, in more of those opportunity-filled rooms more frequently.

Foresight about your prospects and unique relationships that advance your credibility are the legal tender of business development. Each step along the opening path draws on these reserves, requiring a delicate touch of technique and a fistful of finesse.

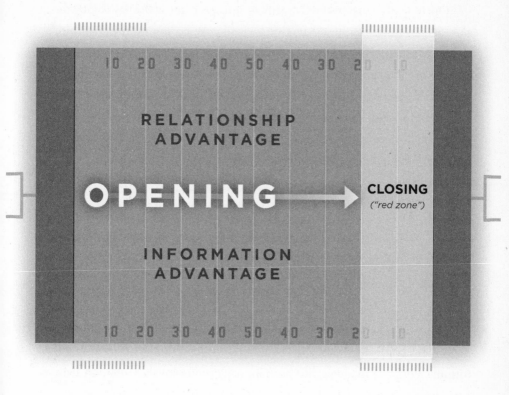

Here's the trick: there is no trickery . . . just authenticity. No manipulation, no game playing, no cheat codes. Success does, however, involve a transformational view of the players on the field. It requires you and your prospective client to get on the same team as early as possible, long before you propose work or are officially hired.

This brings us to another key point:

Your prospect or client is not the opponent. No, the opponent is whatever stands in the way of a prospect's success and the view that anyone but you is capable of and devoted to obliterating the prospect's obstacles.

Opening plays are executed together—prospect and advisor—looking for and then creating openings that advance field position toward the final third and the ultimate goal.

Success also depends on a proven progression of moves. At first glance, the sequence of plays for moving down the field seems simple enough: conduct enough of the right conversations with enough of the right connections often enough and in the right context. Put in an easy-to-tweet way, this would be Opening = Right Connections + Right Conversations + Right Context.

> **OPENING**

Right Connections + Right Conversations + Right Context

However, determining who and what are right is essential but not nearly as simple as it initially seems, and executing consistently and frequently on this formula requires a diligence that escapes many professionals. Common sense is rarely common practice. *The Opening Playbook* provides how-to action steps that will motivate you to persist and succeed.

The Opening Playbook mirrors how a football coach reviews game film and breaks it down play by play to improve players' performance. Watch the footage a play at a time. Stop the film, analyze and discuss the play, and establish plans for executing differently the next time. Watch some more footage. Stop, analyze, discuss, learn, execute. That's how *The Opening Playbook* is arranged.

Our game film—more to the point, our business development story—plays throughout the book. Our story follows six months in the life of Sam Wentworth, a sixth-year associate at a large law firm in a major city. Sam has spent his career to date proving his mettle as an answer-man attorney who in support of his more senior partners completes client engagements with unrelenting drive. (Sound familiar? There's a bit of Sam in all of us.)

Sam stands on the verge of making partner if only he can quickly demonstrate his business development ability. Trouble is, he's never before proved himself in this way, and he's certainly never dealt with pressure to demonstrate his rainmaking chops. The chapters that follow the story thread of Sam and his many unlikely allies who apply the lessons of *The Opening Playbook* start with the opening words "Roll Game Film."

Next, as the story unfolds, we'll stop the film at critical junctures to break down the story situation and provide a how-to framework and specific action steps to help you achieve optimal performance. We will highlight activities that create and sustain openings along with those that prevent entry. These coaching chapters will also help you rely on situational "reads" to modify your actions in the same way a quarterback has to read the situation and possibly call an audible. (For those not conversant with football, an audible is a change of play at the last second, called when the quarterback gets a look at the exact defense he's facing.) Chapters that provide direct instruction and that deliver commentary on the action in Sam's story start with "Coach's Commentary."

"Tactics without strategy is the noise before defeat," Sun Tzu said in his classic text *The Art of War*. Agreed. Aiming before firing is usually a good idea. *The Opening Playbook* puts marketing strategy first. Opening strategy—or positioning, as it is known among marketers—provides roots and grounding for any client development tactics in which you engage. To clarify, there is nothing theoretical about strategy, at least not in *The Opening Playbook*. A theory is abstract reasoning or speculation not necessarily rooted in real-world experience. Strategy is a well-informed plan of action, validated by experience, that increases the likelihood of business development success.

There's no theory in this book.

Everything in *The Opening Playbook* has been battle tested and found to produce significant relationship and revenue gains if it is diligently and sustainably applied. That's because the Opening Strategy approach we will share gives you the ability to crisply answer these questions:

- Who are you?
- What do you do?
- Why should anyone care?
- What are you famous for?

This strategy also serves as your primary decision-making tool for prioritizing the way you spend your business development time most effectively. Perhaps more important than your billable time is your prioritized time.

The key question in today's ever-shifting economy is not "How much time can I bill this client?" but "How else can I spend my time in a way that yields the most value for the client and for me and my firm more quickly?"

Speed matters, and strategy helps you accelerate.

Sun Tzu also said, "Strategy without tactics is the slowest route to victory." Agreed. You'll get plenty of tactical advice from *The Opening Playbook*, too. Steve Ross, the legendary shoot-from-the-hip CEO who transformed the parking garage and funeral home company Kinney National into the media giant Time Warner, claimed that his father had given him the following words of wisdom: There are three categories of people in this world. The first is the individual who wakes up in the morning and goes into the office and proceeds to dream. The second is the individual who gets up in the morning, goes into the office, and proceeds to work 16 hours a day. The third is the individual who comes into the office, dreams for about an hour, and then proceeds to do something about his dreams. You need to go into the third category for only one reason: there's no competition. Figuring your Opening Strategy and planning actions linked to that strategy equate to your hour of dreaming, and this strategy is useful only if you use it to guide the rest of your working day. If your tactics and actions match and support your strategy, you are on the right growth path.

It's time to open your mind. It's time to open relationships and revenue. It's time for a new way of approaching business development. It's time for *The Opening Playbook*.

THE
OPENING
PLAYBOOK

SECTION 1
OPENING PLAYS

DON'T FUMBLE
THE KICKOFF

Roll Game Film

Did you ever have one of those moments when you knew your life was about to change for the better? A moment when all your hard work, all your dedication, and all your effort combined to throw open a new door for your career and all you had to do was walk through? Sam Wentworth was there. He was standing at the threshold.

On this particular morning Sam was a sixth-year associate at the law firm of Habersham & Smith LLP. His legal skills were impeccable; that was what they said in his annual review. They told him that he was on the partnership track, that within a few years he'd be enjoying the profits and perks of that pedigree, a shareholder of a century-old firm with as much prestige and history as any in this city. He just needed to show that he could bring in the work necessary to keep that prestige alive.

The firm's senior partner was a gentleman named Roger Smith. You know the type. He had a Rolodex—yes, he still used a Rolodex—a rotating spindle of business cards the diameter of a basketball. His grandfather had started the firm and passed it down to his boy, and then Roger had inherited it. He'd taken Sam under his wing, showing Sam how he did business.

For Sam, who'd grown up in comfortable but by no means privileged circumstances, Roger's mentorship had been an enlightening experience. The man seemed to know salesmanship like no one Sam had ever met. His motto was "No is not an option." (Granted, he wasn't the most original thinker, but he didn't need to be.) He approached every conversation like the litigator he was, treating it as a closing argument, a sale he hadn't made yet. You wouldn't believe how many stories he could tell about the new clients he'd brought to the firm. Of course, since Sam and his ilk were professional advocates—"We're not used-car peddlers, after all," Roger often said—Roger wouldn't say the word *sales*. But that was what he meant: "You need to be a closer."

Today, Roger had handed Sam the rod and reel to land his first big fish. Sam had gone with other partners to visit clients before, but this time it was a prospect, not a client, and Sam was to do it alone. Joseph Jordan was general counsel with the fastest-growing technology company in the region, Specific Engines. Roger believed that Jordan's company could use a little help negotiating its employment contracts as it expanded, and he'd known Joseph Jordan for as long as he could recall. He gave Sam the rundown on Jordan—wife of 15 years, two kids, Ohio State grad, friendly fellow all the way around. In other words, it was a perfect opportunity for Sam to jump-start his own book of business. Close this deal and it would be partnership dead ahead.

The firm's assistant set up an appointment with Jordan for 3 p.m. on a Tuesday. Perfect time, Roger said, early enough in the week that someone hadn't gotten worn down by the grind but far enough from Monday morning that everyone was already humming and ready to work. "Tuesdays," Roger said, "are when deals get done."

This particular Tuesday was a rainy one, which also boded well. Sure, people were often in a down mood on rainy days, but you could turn that to your advantage. You could bond, stuck inside together, in a way that you can't when minds are wandering on brighter days. As Sam walked into Specific Engines' sleek building, he could see cars and buses sloshing through the downpour, a man huddled in a newsstand smoking a cigar. This was the city, Sam thought, and soon it would be *his* city.

Sam already had a bit of skill with people. Charm, one might say. And he thought on his feet as well as anyone. Though he was still in his early thirties, he believed that he knew enough about enough things that he could jump in the deep water of anyone's pool. He believed he didn't need to spend a whole lot of time preparing for a client meeting—and yes, he was already envisioning Specific Engines as a client, because that's what closers do. As he rode the elevator up 26 floors to the company's downtown offices, he thought about how he'd present himself to Jordan, and he started getting the tiniest bit nervous.

He checked his reflection in the gleaming doors of the elevator. Every hair in place, suit crisp even after the rain, teeth gleaming. Sam wasn't knockout handsome, but he had the look of a best friend from college, a familiar haven't-I-met-you-before appearance.

Once in the waiting room, Sam looked around, trying to discern clues to what the company's executives valued by the kinds of decor they'd chosen for their walls, the kinds of magazines that rested on the coffee table. The furniture was angular, minimalist; the art was . . . well, nothing that he could readily identify. Hues and tones and swipes and shapes. The magazines were the standard mix of news, finance, and sports with a couple of avant-garde architectural publications in the mix. Sam couldn't find anything relatable to latch on to.

Quickly, he took out his phone and called up the day's headlines. Strife in the Middle East . . . the Dow up 10 points early . . . striking workers at the city's civic center. He tried his best to take it all in to have something to talk about.

"Mr. Wentworth?" The receptionist's voice startled Sam, and he jumped ever so slightly. "Sorry. Mr. Jordan will see you now."

Sam tucked his phone into his pocket, rose, and straightened his suit jacket. He paused only long enough to say Roger's mantra in his head—"No is not an option"—and followed the receptionist through Specific Engines' corridors. As he walked, he tried to focus on anything distinctive he could notice to help him get an edge, an *in*, with Jordan. This was his moment, this was huge, this could make his career—and then, before Sam knew it, he was at Jordan's door.

"Mr. Wentworth!" Jordan said from within the office. "Come in, come in." He extended a hand in greeting, and Sam remembered the lessons his father had given him—firm grip, two pumps, look a man in the eye. Done. Jordan returned the handshake and motioned for Sam to take a seat.

"You come highly recommended from Roger," Jordan said. "How is he, by the way? I haven't seen him since you had that Christmas party at the City Club . . . was that two years ago?"

"I believe so, sir. He's doing very well. Very busy. As a matter of fact, that's why he sent me to you. He believes that I could do a fine job of representing your business in some of your—"

Jordan put his hands up. "Whoa, whoa, slow down there, Sam. We'll get to that." He turned to the receptionist, who was still standing in the doorway. "Amanda, would you mind getting us something to drink? Sam, what can she bring you?"

Sam tried to think. It was after lunch, but was it too early to have a drink? Should he have a drink? Or should he go with water? A soda? Too late in the day for coffee. . . . "Whatever you're having," he finally said.

"Two bottled waters," Jordan said, and then, as if reading Sam's uncertainty, "This isn't *Mad Men*. You ever see that show?"

"Now and then," Sam said, hoping Jordan wouldn't press the point. "I don't watch a whole lot of television. Movies are more my thing." Sam let the bait hang, and Jordan bit.

"That so? What have you seen lately?"

"The new James Bond film was a lot of fun. Keeps your interest for the whole film. Can't say that about many movies today."

"I used to love James Bond!" Jordan said, and Sam felt a surge of satisfaction. "What do you think of the new guy? I was always a Connery fan myself." There we go. A glimmer of light. Keep going.

"The new guy is great!" Sam said, his voice steadier than it had been all day. "When I was a kid, I used to think that Roger Moore was the best. It's only now, when you get older, that you realize gimmicks aren't the heart of the James Bond franchise; it's the style and the cool. But there was this one time in *Moonraker* where—"

Jordan had been listening politely, but as Sam began talking the minutiae of James Bond movies, he shifted visibly in his seat. Sam recognized the sign. "Control the conversation," Roger had said. It was slipping away.

"We can talk about this the next time we get together," Sam said. "I'm sure you're very busy."

"Would rather be talking James Bond, to be honest," he said. "But we still have a little work to get done today, right?"

"We do. And I'm glad you said that, because—" Sam started to reach into his briefcase and pull out a portfolio of his credentials.

"Boy, you don't mess around, do you, Sam? I'd like to see what you brought, but let's talk a little more first. Tell me a bit about yourself. Give me the biography of Sam Wentworth."

Breathe, Sam thought. Breathe. You've got him on your side. Don't lose him. "Well, I went to undergrad at Michigan, which I hope you won't hold against me, being from Ohio State and all." Jordan nodded at Sam with a smile. So far, so good. "I've been in practice for three years. My specialties include employment law and—"

"Kids?"

That threw Sam. "Sir?"

"Joe. Call me Joe. Do you have kids, Sam? A family?"

"Not yet, sir, but someday. Still not married either. I'm sure your two keep you very busy."

He smiled again, but this time it lacked warmth. "Three, Sam. I have three kids."

"Really?"

"Really. It's not a puppy that's kept me up most of the last six months, I can assure you."

Sam's mind raced as if he were slipping on ice. Roger's information was out of date! Third kid? At Jordan's age? Was he on to spouse number two? Sam's thoughts were scrambling. . . . Should he ask? Maybe his new wife was a lot younger than Jordan was. What else had Roger gotten wrong? What else did Sam need to remember about Jordan, and was that wrong too?

Again Jordan seemed to sense Sam's discomfort. "Sam," he said, bringing Sam out of his head, "let's see what you've got there."

Sam handed him the portfolio, grateful for an opportunity to move on from his stomach-churning embarrassment.

Jordan flipped through the portfolio, a collection of his résumé, his legal writing and court opinions in his favor, and his firm's marketing brochures. For long minutes the only sound in the office was that of turning pages. Sam tried to stifle a cough and could not. Jordan looked up at him and closed the folder.

"This is wonderful and I'm very glad you brought it," he said, tapping on the folder's cover, "but I'm not exactly in the market for new outside counsel. We're doing just fine on our own with our in-house team."

"I'm sure that's true, sir, but let me take a moment to tell you the many ways in which I could help you." Sam sat up straighter in his chair and began his prepared speech. "I offer my clients unparalleled drive, the resources of one of the state's top firms, a willingness to go the extra mile and—"

Jordan started laughing. *Laughing!* It wasn't a cruel laugh, but it was a laugh nonetheless, and Sam felt his stomach drop. "Is this a commercial? Sam, relax. I'm sure you're very good at what you do, but at the moment I just can't use you."

No is not an option, Sam reminded himself. "How many employment lawsuits are you a party to right now?"

The laugh vanished. "Excuse me?" Jordan said.

Sam felt the faintest curl of cold creeping around his gut but pushed onward, expecting that he, like James Bond, could outrun any impending explosion. "How many new hire contracts does your team have in front of you right now? I could certainly help with—"

"We don't share that information, Sam," Jordan said. Sam recognized the tone in his voice but kept pushing. Maybe, just maybe, he could push right past this and get back into Jordan's good graces. Everyone likes persistence, after all, right?

"I understand that, and of course you wouldn't," Sam said. "Roger told me you're growing fast, and, well, I'm not suggesting that you can't handle what you have. . . . I'm just saying that perhaps you could handle what you have a little bit better."

"Really," he said. "And why would you think that?"

"Well, it's easy to drop balls when things are moving so fast. And a lot of times we're so close to our contract negotiations that we miss things others with fresh eyes can catch."

"That's why we already have five lawyers in house, Sam. And we're about to hire a sixth."

"Sure, sure," Sam said, and he could hear his voice getting higher. He stopped for a second to bring himself back under control. "I'm sure they're all very good. Why would they be here if they weren't, right? What I'm saying is that if we worked together, we could all benefit. Would you mind if I took a look at one of your employment agreements? I bet I can find some ways to improve it."

Jordan smiled and looked out the window at the rain. Then he stood, put Sam's folder on his desk, and extended his hand. "It was a pleasure to meet you, Sam. Please give my best to Roger, all right?"

Sam took his hand and shook it, though his grip wasn't nearly as strong as before. "Sir?"

"Thank you for coming in, Sam," he said, and then looked to the door. "Oh, here's our water. Sam was just leaving, Amanda."

"I—ah—" Sam tried to compose himself even though both Jordan and Amanda had made it clear that it was time for him to go. "So . . . we should meet for dinner sometime soon. We can talk a little more James Bond."

"That'd be lovely. Check with my assistant to set it up."

"Sir." Sam stopped at the door, Roger's mantra pounding in his head. "I'd really like the opportunity to work with you and your colleagues. I really think we have something to offer your organization, and I feel like I didn't get that across here."

"Sam," Jordan said, putting a hand on the young attorney's shoulder, "it's my experience that I almost never have to use the word *no*, because most people know when a conversation is headed that way already. You already know, Sam, but just so there's no doubt . . ."

Sam felt his insides curl up. He knew what was coming.

"... No." He slapped Sam genially on the back, a slap with the slightest bit of a push behind it.

As his stomach dropped to the soles of his feet, Sam got the message. Loud and clear.

Sam left without a word to the receptionist. Later, he would say it felt as if he just appeared down in the lobby so many floors below, rain pelting down onto the sidewalk out front.

What had just happened? How had everything turned out so wrong? Sure, he didn't know how many kids Jordan had, and he might have been a little aggressive in going for his business, but wasn't that what he was supposed to do?

Outside, everything was exactly the same. The rain was still falling. The cars and buses and cabs were still running. The newsstand proprietor was still smoking his cigar. But for Sam everything had changed completely. The rain no longer felt like a good omen, the clouds seemed darker, and the puddles were deeper than he remembered when he'd arrived less than 30 minutes ago.

How could Sam face Roger now? How could he go back into the office, knowing he'd failed? Roger would make it clear: Sam had not just let him down, he'd let his entire *firm* down. Roger couldn't care less about how Sam felt. His concern would be for the reputation—and revenue—of the firm. And Sam knew exactly what he would say about this afternoon. This was not good.

Sam couldn't go back to the office. He just couldn't. There was no way. Not yet. He needed time: time to collect himself, time to figure out what had gone wrong. In Specific Engines' building there was a behemoth coffee shop, a space so huge that it seemed more like an auto dealership. It was a caffeine factory. A line of people ran out the door and into the lobby: a line of people who all looked exactly like Sam.

Hardly soothing. Sam needed solitude. He needed space to think.

Sam stepped outside into the deluge. Down the street he could see rays of warm light from another shop cutting through the driving rain.

He moved rapidly toward the light. He laughed humorlessly at this hallucination. Maybe, he thought, I'm having a near-death experience.

As Sam sloshed through sidewalk puddles, though, the mirage turned out to be real. The shop's corner windows were stenciled with intricate drawings of coffee cups and cupcakes as well as laptops and cell phones. Inside, he could see people sipping at coffee cups but also working away in a quiet, calm setting. The place was called The Open Note. Sam didn't know if it had decent food or coffee, and at this point he didn't care. If they were functioning in this economy, they were doing something right, something better than what he was doing.

Sam pulled his coat up over his head and trudged through the downpour toward the light.

ESTABLISH FIELD POSITION

2

Coach's Commentary

Let's stop the film here because it's just too painful to continue. Actually, at this point, if we think of reading Sam's story in terms of watching game film, it's like reviewing first-day footage of a terrible team like the Bad News Bears. There are so many issues to address that it's hard to know where to begin. Let's look first at the overarching matter: Sam's intention.

Sam was intent on closing a deal in the first meeting despite never having earned the right to do so. Sam went on the offensive way too early, and as a result he was, well, offensive.

> The idea of an initial prospect conversation isn't to win the business on the spot; it's to engage in a conversation that establishes your right to talk further and explore ways to provide support to the prospect.

In football terms, instead of trying to fling a Hail Mary on the first play, Sam would have done better to find his comfort zone and figure out a strategy to work his way down the field. You've got to be in the game and on the field before you can score.

The word *opening* seemed not to be in Sam's vocabulary, and even if it was, he might have misunderstood its manifold relevance to his situation. Words and actions can be open to multiple interpretations; such is the nature of human interaction. How would Sam's approach to Joe Jordan have differed if he'd considered the varieties of opening?

As an adjective, *opening* refers to the beginning of something new. The opening play on a football field is a quarterback's first of the game. What if, instead of closing a deal, Sam's intention for his first meeting with Jordan had been simply to begin what might well become a long-term personal and professional relationship rather than a transaction to be closed ASAP? He would have taken the pressure off himself and the situation, allowing for a more natural flow of dialogue and connection. He would have had a chance for a next meeting.

What if he had said something along the lines of "Mr. Jordan, my goal for our meeting today is simply to introduce myself and to begin a dialogue. You don't know me yet, and I haven't earned the right to expect anything more. I don't come empty-handed. I can share my observations and hypotheses about how your competitors are handling certain litigious situations and what that might mean for Specific Engines. And I would welcome hearing how you perceive the same situations and what else may be a priority for your team. That way, I can keep my eyes and ears open for ways to be supportive going forward."

When the word *opening* is used as a verb—as in to open up and talk freely—it means to reveal oneself in an increasingly straightforward and uninhibited way. If Sam had embraced this version of opening, he would have worried less about being perceived as a peer to Roger and Jordan and been more genuine and approachable. What if Sam had said something that acknowledged his vulnerability and the imbalance of experience, knowledge, and power in the room? "Mr. Jordan, I can't hide the fact that I'm still early in my career. I think that's why Roger asked me to visit with you in particular. He knows your reputation for taking chances on smart young talent with an entrepreneurial work ethic and lots of curiosity. The truth is, you get a lot for your money that way: letting a partner-track associate serve you. He knows, too, that I would gain as much as I give in supporting your efforts because of your expertise not just as a savvy client but also as a skillful coach. But again, that's just my guess. My expectation today is just to open what I hope will be a long-term business friendship. Does that align with what you were expecting, or was there something else you wanted to make sure we cover?"

As a noun, *opening* can mean a gap or hole through which you can squeeze from one situation to another. In this first encounter with a senior executive recommended by Sam's senior partner, humility and attentive listening might have allowed Sam to see an opening through which he could have shifted his status from an unknown entity to a known one on the path to being liked and trusted by the prospect. Sam found some relationship daylight in his James Bond affinity with Jordan, but if that conversation cracked open a relationship door, Sam closed it on his foot in the next breath. He didn't need to keep yapping about action films, but neither was it time for him to whip out his credentials. In transitioning from the James Bond conversation, Sam might have said, "Well, now you know something about my cinematic interests and experience. Would it be helpful if I told you something about my professional experience? Who knows, maybe we'll find more common ground."

One more way to define the word *opening* is as the process of clarifying, unfolding, broadening, revealing, making more responsive, and understanding. Aren't those the actions involved in developing a productive business advisory relationship? How might Sam have behaved differently if he had made this flavor of opening his first and ongoing priority in his relationship with Jordan?

Enough with the vocabulary lessons. Let's now take in order the hard lessons (myths?) Sam thought he should have learned by now and how they all failed to materialize:

No is not an option. That didn't work at all. Jordan told Sam in no uncertain terms that no was his *only* option.

Know your client. Sam *did* know the client. Sure, he could have learned a bit more about his family and he did discover a James Bond commonality, but it turns out that relying on a few small talk tricks wasn't enough.

Control the conversation. Jordan immediately sensed manipulation in Sam's attempt to control the conversation. He was spending too much time controlling and not enough being present and listening.

Close the deal. Well, we saw how well that went.

Sam got it wrong in a more foundational way, though. He had never met Joe Jordan before, yet he was expecting to close a deal before he had opened a relationship. In business development, an opening is an opportunity to deliver real value to a prospect or client—and to demonstrate what it's like to work with you—before you are hired to do so.

Here are several lessons that would have served Sam better than the ones he learned from Roger.

TRY OPENING BEFORE CLOSING

Perhaps this is common sense, but it certainly is not common practice. Opening is the business development equivalent of baseball's moneyball, the strategy employed by Oakland A's visionary Billy Beane. The A's learned that they won more, while holding the line on staffing costs, when they hired players who had a high likelihood of getting on base when they were up to bat. The more bases per at bat, the better. Progression up the field or around the bases makes a difference even if not every single possession results in points or runs. Similarly, there is a time and place for moving from business friendship to the idea of working together with a client and from there to actually being engaged to do the work. Especially early in a business relationship, the goal is not to elicit a yes or no response but to open the dialogue and to demonstrate the business value that you bring to the budding relationship.

Once you've earned the right, you may ask, "How would you like to proceed? May I draft a proposal describing how my firm and I will approach this challenge and support your efforts?" But if you're hoping for a trusted advisory business relationship that goes beyond one transactional encounter, the time to close is rarely, if ever, during the first meeting.

Unlike in football, a true professional relationship often doesn't have a set end zone but rather a set of continual openings to broader opportunity.

PREPARE TO OPEN, NOT TO MANIPULATE

Sam prides himself on being able to strike up a conversation with anyone, but all too often he relies on that gift of gab in lieu of actual preparation. With opening rather than closing as the goal, Sam would have prepared differently for his meeting with Jordan. Reading over someone's LinkedIn profile isn't nearly enough. You don't need to be a stalker, but you do need to have a sense of who someone is so that you can start to understand what you can do for that person. What did Sam know about Jordan's position and career goals and aspirations and how he and his team would be evaluated this year? What did Sam know about Specific Engines' marketplace, its top strategic initiatives, its biggest threats and opportunities? Virtually nothing, and it showed.

Rather than making opening statements that were based on his research, with slightly modified preparation Sam could have offered curiosity-based opening questions, observations, and hypotheses for discussion. He would not presume to know it all. It's far more important to come in with an open mind and deep, genuine curiosity about your prospect and his or her business. Of course, that too is useless if you're in the wrong place altogether. There was a more fundamental question that Sam could have asked himself and Roger: Were Joe Jordan and Specific Engines the right contact and target for Sam

Wentworth to pursue? (We'll examine that question together with you in Chapters 8 and 10.)

OPEN OTHER POSSIBLE OPTIONS BEYOND YES OR NO

Sam was engulfed by one of the paradoxes of trying to be both a trusted advisor and a rainmaker.

> Professionals need a constant flow of new client work, and this requires us to market with a sense of urgency. At the same time we must establish trust with our prospective clients, and rushing relationships is a great way to contaminate trust.

Leaving room for only one good outcome to a business development encounter introduces undue stress into the situation. "No is not an option" is an absurdly limited idea. It produces a binary situation—you get either a yes or a no outcome. Instead, what you want is a possibility-filled outcome that leads to another opportunity to build your value and trust in the mind of the prospect. Before your next critical business development meeting, brainstorm a range of possible positive options and outcomes besides yes or no.

One of the most important questions to ask yourself is "How else?" To wit:

How else can I perceive this person and this meeting?

How else can I approach this in a way in which, right from the start, my prospect and I are playing on the same side of the field, on the same team?

How else can we be of help to each other beyond him buying something from me right now?

OPEN WITH ENTHUSIASM, NOT DESPERATION

To some degree, client development in professional services is a numbers game. The more credible referrals and on-target prospects you have, the more likely it is that a client engagement will emerge at any particular time. Everyone you connect with in some way may be of help to you professionally. You just never know who knows whom and how your encounter with a person may boomerang to benefit or bite you. Thus, each conversation you have matters; each one carries opening potential.

At the same time, when we approach any given contact with the sense that our job depends on successfully "closing" an engagement with him or her, we are apt to behave in a way that destroys trust. Somehow, our anxiety about the situation surfaces directly or subtly, and our discussions shift for the worse. If you are a "premature closer," you position yourself opposite your prospective client, persuading the client to buy something he or she may not need. If you are a patient opener, you figuratively sit on the same side of the table with your prospects, working together to solve their business issues.

Instead of my-life-depends-on-this-sale thinking, imagine (whether or not it may be true) that it really doesn't matter whether this one project comes through. You've got plenty to keep you going. If it isn't this one, it will be the next. You would love to work with this prospect because you know you can make a difference. But if this one doesn't come through, it's okay. It's not mission-critical. If, in fact, any one potential engagement is going to make or break you or your firm, it's probably time to find another firm or another profession.

Enter each encounter with the underlying sense that this one discussion isn't so desperately essential. By all means, feel free to tell your prospects that you like them and their businesses and would love to work with them. But focus your attention not on the winning or losing of the "sale" but rather on being a great client advisor and opening the relationship.

NAIL THE OPENING SERIES

3

Roll Game Film

There's something about a fire and a hearth that just puts you at ease immediately, isn't there? Something about safety and security and warmth that has passed from the dawn of humankind to the iPhone era. As soon as Sam walked into The Open Note, the fireplace in the center of the shop drew his eye. It was a large multisided fireplace encircled by a wrought-iron grate and surrounded by thick leather chairs and couches. Sam had never seen so many windows in a coffee joint before— enormous and warehouse loft style, no less—enveloping the room and allowing the soft light of a rainy day to wash over everything. The shop sat on a corner, and that had the dual effect of making it visible from almost any angle on four blocks and making it feel open and airy once you were inside. This was a place to gather and to gather oneself. Sam had stumbled on the perfect spot to hide out.

Just then, the most delightful aroma he could imagine wafted up to him: warm chocolate chip cookies, the milk chocolate still soft in the dough. And they were on a plate held right in front of him.

"You look like you could use one of these," said the woman holding the plate, a genial glint in her eye. "Nothing in the world a warm cookie can't fix."

He scooped two off the plate and had three bites down before he stopped to look at her. She was young, maybe only a few years older than Sam, if that.

Dark hair, bright eyes. She was petite—mildly pretty in a plain, girl-next-door way—but when she stood there with one hand on her hip and a thousand-watt smile, she could have been Wonder Woman. She had this indefinable . . . something. Presence? That was it. She had *presence*. "Sorry," Sam said. "How much?"

The woman gave the second you-have-to-be-kidding look Sam had gotten in the last half hour. "No charge, my friend."

"No charge? Really? These cookies would be three bucks apiece up the street."

She smiled. "I'm not going to turn away your money if you want to pay me for the cookies," she said, "but they're compliments of the house." She extended her hand. "I'm Candace."

"Sam Wentworth," Sam said, shaking her hand, and then the obvious occurred to him. "You work here, I guess."

"Something like that. I started The Open Note. I'm the owner . . . the boss lady, I guess you could say. Come on in, sit, sit."

Sam finally took a moment to look around the shop. Radiating out from that central fireplace were tables and soft chairs dotted with customers. Some were on laptops, others on their phones, others reading books, others chatting. But unlike other coffee shops he'd frequented, which tended to be frenetic and impersonal, everyone here seemed to know everyone else, or at least they acted as if they did; people smiled and said hello. The prevailing mood was one of calm, connection. If The Open Note had a motto, it would have been "Check your stress at the door."

Warm jazz flowed from the speakers overhead, and the fire's heat radiated throughout the room. Photographs and paintings decorated the walls of the shop, and Sam noticed that each one had a tiny price tag on it. Sam found his eyes drawn to a small painting on one wall, a sailboat on the water not far from shore. As subject matter went, it was clichéd; as far as execution, it was folk art at best—broad brushstrokes, cartoonish images, vibrant colors that seemed to come from cans of house paint.

This painting wouldn't have graced a dark closet in Jordan's office. Still, there was something about it that intrigued Sam: something genuine, raw, and approachable. Sam *understood* this art.

"You like the painting," Candace said. "An art aficionado, are you?"

"I try to look out for anything interesting," Sam said. "Not enough money yet to be a collector."

"There's art for any budget," she said, turning over the price tag: $150. "Self-taught artist. Quite a character. Captain Durrell Barnard. Shell-shocked war veteran—navy. I don't think he's held a real job for decades. He lives in what he calls Heaven Harbor on a ramshackle boat docked on the swampy outskirts of Lake Carson. I swear—I couldn't make this up. The whole thing—boat, dock, everything the man owns—he has decorated with boating scenes and poems about the water. It's really something. Looks like it was built from scraps he found in the woods or on the side of the road—bottles, furniture, sinks, car parts. His neighbors with the multimillion-dollar lake houses aren't too happy about him . . . think he's just a nut. But I think the joke is on them and his art will be worth a bundle once his work and his story get out."

"Interesting," Sam said with mild interest, then looked to the counter. "Do I order up there?"

She smiled and stayed silent a beat longer than necessary. "I can take your order, hon. What can I bring you?"

"Just coffee. Black."

"Coffee black it is," she said, turning to return to the kitchen.

Sam found a seat near the fire and saw a crisp menu sitting on the chair's expansive arm. He flipped through it, then noticed something interesting: there were Open Notes in seven states. Seven! How had he not heard of this place? And how had someone . . . well, no offense to her, but how had someone like Candace, who looked more hugs-and-kisses than Harvard Business School, managed to keep stores thriving in seven states? He fired up his phone to check her out and had just begun to see the many angles of The Open Note—coffee shops, food trucks, catering—when the coffee arrived.

Sam reached for his wallet, but Candace held up one hand. "Pay me when you're ready to leave." She smiled. "You look like you could use a few minutes to relax."

"Just a few," Sam said, blowing on the coffee. "I'll be on my way in just a sec. Needed to warm up."

"Wise idea." She nodded and began collecting a couple of plates near him. "What on earth took you outside on such a miserable day? You should have been in here all day long."

"If only I'd known you were here before!" Sam smiled and immediately felt guilty. He might have just torpedoed his career, after all. This was no time to be smiling.

Candace saw the smile fade. "Tough afternoon?"

"The toughest," Sam said. "I might have just flushed my career down the toilet."

"Sounds like that might not be the worst thing in the world," Candace said, and Sam looked at her, uncertain. "Things we treasure don't often end up in the toilet, do they?" She smiled and looked around. "Sorry. Probably not the best subject matter to discuss around food, is it?"

Candace had an aura about her that made Sam smile even though he couldn't have imagined he'd smile again this day. She had a curious combination of innocence and experience that made him want to get to know her better and also tell her about himself.

"What do you do, Sam Wentworth?" Candace asked, as if reading his mind.

"I'm an attorney."

"Ah." She nodded knowingly. "But that's not who you *are*, is it? Tell me about you. Where are you from?"

Sam realized it was the same line of questioning Joseph Jordan had pursued. But this time Sam didn't have a convenient script prepared. He didn't know anything about Candace beyond the fact that she seemed to run an extremely pleasant coffee shop.

Her agenda, if she had any at all, seemed solely to make
him comfortable. So he talked.

He talked about growing up in Chicago, about wanting to avoid his father's erratic path chasing one crazy venture after another, about his pursuit of law—something that seemed more predictable to him—about school at

Michigan, about learning his way around this city. He talked about his hopes and fears for his career and his uncertainty about what would happen now, after the Jordan debacle. And when he'd finished, he realized he'd spent a good ten minutes of Candace's time, but she didn't appear to be in any way rushed.

"And now you're here," she said as the story reached her front door.

"And now I'm here," Sam agreed. "Sorry to take so much of your time."

"No apologies necessary," Candace said, getting to her feet. "Tuesday afternoons are a good time for meeting new friends and having wide open conversations." It wasn't lost on Sam that this was the exact opposite of Roger's advice.

As Sam considered how likely Roger would be to dismiss this little shop and its bubbly owner, his eye focused for the first time on the translucent tinted glass wall that separated the café from a much larger space beyond. There seemed to be a hearth glowing on the other side. Sam could faintly see workspaces, desks, even a conference room. He saw movement. A door inconspicuously cut in the glass opened into the café. A young man in a blue blazer and jeans stepped in, spoke a few words to the barista, and used his key card to slip back through the door to what was apparently an alternative universe on the other side. Sam thought it curious, but he was too busy contemplating his own sorrows to give it much consideration. *Unless someone over there can hand me some new business,* he thought, *they could be running a brothel back there for all I care.*

Before long, Sam knew it was time to go and stood to gather his materials. Candace noticed him and swung by. "I enjoyed making a new friend today . . . that's you, by the way. I think you'll find a lot of kindred spirits here. We are going to see you in here again, right?" The question struck Sam with both its expectation and its anticipation.

"Of course," Sam said before he even knew what he was saying. "That would be nice," he continued, though he had absolutely no intention of being back anytime soon. Coffee shop chat was one thing, but he had no time for or interest in new friendships these days. He needed new clients, not buddies. He pulled a few bills out of his pocket, left them on the table, and turned to go. For just a moment he looked again at the sailboat painting, wishing he could be on an idyllic cruise on the Mediterranean rather than heading back into the rain and his faltering legal career.

"You like that piece, don't you?" Candace said. "I understand. There's nothing more inspiring than an authentic expression of raw creativity."

"Um, yeah . . . it's nice," Sam said, feigning nonchalance in an attempt to avoid the sales pitch he felt certain was coming next.

Sure, it was interesting enough. And no, a hundred fifty bucks wasn't too much to spend on some poor local artist's work. In fact, the painting really was growing on him. And if that stuff about living on an old junk boat was true, there was a pretty cool story behind it. But just as Sam started to feel the artist's story tug at his emotions, he felt the stronger, more familiar pull of old habits tugging at him, reminding him that there would be no immediate benefit from buying that particular piece of art.

Besides, what if the story was really just a bunch of hype meant to lure suckers like him into buying the emperor's clothes? He had read recently about a famous sports memorabilia entrepreneur who bought a T206 Honus Wagner baseball card for $25,000 and sold it a couple of years later for $110,000, claiming that it was the genuine article: a rare specimen kept in mint condition. Hockey star Wayne Gretzky and a partner later bought the coveted card for over $450,000. A few transactions later, the card sold again—this time for $2.8 million. More recently, Sam learned, the collector who started the frenzy had pleaded guilty to fraud for altering the card to make it look better and massively raise its value. Authenticity isn't always what it appears to be.

"You know what they say," Sam quipped. "Authenticity is the key to success. If you can fake that, you've got it made."

Candace smiled, nodding as if she understood. "Yes, that happens all too often—I've heard it referred to as fauxthenticity. Go visit the artist sometime and you'll see for yourself. In the meanwhile, come on back tomorrow. Maybe that boat will still be here. Maybe there'll be something you like better. No worries either way."

She held the door open for Sam, and the gray day seemed even less inviting than before. But it was time for him to go.

"See you soon, Candace," he said.

"Hope so, Sam," she replied.

As he walked up the block, Sam tried to deduce why Candace's shop had been so inviting. But he didn't have much time to dwell on that. He had one more lead, one more chance to put Roger's lessons into play. He would hold off today; he would give himself time to decompress, to focus on billing hours instead of selling them. He would make the call tomorrow morning, and with any luck Candace would be nothing more than a pleasant diversion. Of course, if this next call didn't go well, Sam realized he might be back at Candace's by lunchtime . . . looking for a job.

ESTABLISH QUARTERBACK- RECEIVER RHYTHM

4

Coach's Commentary

Who was really responsible for the difficult conversation between Sam and Joe Jordan? Who matters more in connecting for a successful pass, the quarterback or the receiver? It doesn't matter. They aren't competitors; they're teammates. What matters is that the quarterback and the receiver have built a trusting relationship over time and have established a rhythm of working together on the field.

In the same way, Sam (and you and me and everyone) needs to establish a relationship rhythm with his prospects—a steady give-and-take of ideas and value—before he can expect much movement up the business development playing field.

Let's look at how Candace approached her first encounter with Sam as an example. She doesn't perceive Sam as a customer as much as she sees him as a guest in her home and a potential friend. And she definitely doesn't treat Sam like a competitor, someone she has to outflank, subdue, capture, and trick into doing something he doesn't really want to do. Her first focus and intention was to understand what Sam was all about and to learn what stood in the way of his happiness. Only then could she bring whatever resources she and The Open Note could muster to Sam's aid.

Candace knows that someone has to feel comfortable before opening up and that the best way to facilitate that is to create an open environment and be open yourself first. In starting a business relationship, as in approaching an unfamiliar dog, if you approach in a threatening manner, you may get bitten. If you approach a strange hound with your palm down or your fist clenched, coming suddenly from above as if to whack it on the head, the dog is likely to snap. In contrast, if you approach with your palm open, facing upward and moving slowly from below as if you will feed the dog, you usually get a better response. The safety of a genuine and generous open hand—that's the tone and context Candace has created for first impressions. This behavior needs to be repeated with each early encounter to build recognition and receptivity.

We are so oversaturated with sales hype in today's always-on media-drenched world that most prospects are conditioned to expect a self-interested sales pitch from whoever approaches them. Therefore, we can't expect prospects to believe a word we say no matter how sincerely it is delivered, at least not at first. Sam's cynical dismissal of the folk art painting is a good example of this. Candace was merely describing to Sam something that appeared to be of interest to him. Sam read it as a sales pitch and closed down. Candace recognized his withdrawal and indicated that whether Sam bought the art or not, it was all the same to her. She understands that authenticity is too often faked. She also knows that authenticity can't ultimately be described; it can only be experienced. And she's been doing her best to demonstrate hers.

Candace needs Sam and her other customers to serve as her army of evangelists in her competition against the giant coffee shop chains. Before that can happen, Candace's customers need to repeatedly engage with her, enjoy her support, and experience firsthand her authentic value. Thus, she proceeds with patience, giving others time to ponder and process their interactions with her and to conclude on their own that she is genuinely available to help them succeed. She knows that a relationship must begin somewhere, though, and takes care to ensure a great starting point. Here are four attributes of Candace's first-encounter behavior that made Sam a receptive recruit.

FINDABLE

The Open Note was intentionally designed with oversized windows not only to ensure an open, cheery interior but also to enable the facility to be a beacon. Remember that Sam was attracted first by "rays of warm light from another shop cutting through the driving rain." It was easy to find once he was in appropriate range. Once he was inside, Candace swiftly, smoothly made sure that Sam knew who she was and demonstrated her value to him from the start. How can the right prospective clients find you? What's your beacon of light drawing prospects to you? Having enough of the right connections is one of the key components of opening new client relationships. We'll learn more about this in Section 3.

FRIENDLY

In our time-pressed business world, key encounters need to move to fact-based conversations rather quickly. However, most of us move too quickly and ignore the fact that we're interacting with unpredictable humans, not programmable robots. Business relationships actually advance faster if we start by recognizing the personal feelings and career interests of our counterparts. Candace gets it. She read Sam's body language, saw he was in pain, and approached him with warmth and empathy. Friendly is the right attitude to begin a new connection. Friendly is an attitude of feeling first and facts next.

Fake friendly is readily transparent and makes you suspect.
Friendly for real, as in authentically curious about others,
makes you likable.

Whom do we like? We like people who genuinely like us. Consider your next key prospect encounter. What sparks your curiosity about the person, not just the business, you will be meeting? What is it about that business and especially that particular person that you already like on the basis of the research you've done? How will you express that friendly enthusiasm in the first meeting? We'll talk about conducting conversations that enhance trust and likability in Section 4.

FREE

You've got to give to get, says the common pay-it-forward wisdom. Why should anyone spend time with you if it is evident the agenda is all yours? Demonstrate immediately that you are bringing something of value to the other person. It doesn't have to be grand; it does have to be freely given. For Candace, it was a batch of warm chocolate chip cookies. You can never go wrong with chocolate, but in a new client development encounter, bring something of business value first. In your next key prospect encounter, how will you leave that executive better off even if that company never hires you? We'll talk about how to provide samples of your work before you are hired in Section 4.

FORWARD

Candace opened her relationship with Sam with the long term in mind. Sam sensed the positive expectation and anticipation she felt in his imminent return. Although she surely wanted Sam to return because repeat customers are good business, there was more there. He could tell that she truly enjoyed his company and wanted to help him. A quarterback and a receiver need to have time on the field together—preferably in game situations—to build rhythm. That doesn't happen in the first practice or the first game but through consistent, continuous interaction over time, getting better as each encounter occurs and progresses. In your next prospect encounter, how are you going to ensure that there is a next time? We'll talk about how you can keep a good relationship going over the long haul in Section 6.

DEVELOP POCKET PRESENCE

5

Roll Game Film

The next day dawned bright and sunny, and Sam chose to see that as symbolic. He returned to the law firm's stately offices fired up from his visit to The Open Note, and he made a mental note to send Candace some flowers when he landed his next big client. It seemed the least he could do.

Sam's office was in the interior ring of his floor; windows were for partners. Sam could see the sunlight from their windows reflecting off his door. Not for the first time—not for the hundredth—he vowed to secure that window, to look out over the city from his very own office.

He began the morning with some routine e-mail correspondence and to-do list management, but as the hours wore on, he realized what he was dreading: the call from Roger. Shortly before noon—probably about the time Roger strolled into the office—it came.

Roger was in the middle of carping at his secretary when Sam picked up the phone. Sam waited while Roger reoriented himself to the task at hand and began to talk.

"All right. Give me the story on Jordan."

Sam felt his stomach curl in on itself. "Ah . . . it didn't go so well, sir."

"Didn't go so well? What does that mean? Either it goes or it doesn't go."

"Then," Sam said, breathing in, "it didn't go."

Roger exhaled then, the kind of sigh a parent makes when a child has screwed up the simplest overexplained task. "Fine. What do you have today?"

"I have to prepare for a depo—"

"Wrong. The right answer is, 'Nothing, Mr. Smith. What would you like me to do today?'"

Sam paused and realized that Roger actually wanted him to repeat the line. "Nothing, Mr. Smith. What would you like me to do today?" Sam's eyes were clenched shut hard enough to cause a headache.

"I want you to land a client; that's what I want," Roger said. Sam heard Roger rustling around on his desk for something, and then the voice came back on the line, annoyed and rushed. "Alex Itzikoff. Universal Airlines. I told you about this a week ago." He barked out a number. "They need quality counsel. Make the call."

"I'll get right to it, sir," Sam said. The call had already been on his agenda for the day.

"See that you do," Roger said, and the phone rattled as if he had dropped it from a good foot above the receiver.

Sam stared at the number on his notepad, breathed deeply, and punched in the number. After a couple rings, a woman's voice answered. He wasn't sure whether he had dialed the main number or a direct line. The voice gave him no clue.

"Hello, this is Sam Wentworth with Habersham & Smith. I'm calling for Alex Itzikoff on the recommendation of my colleague Roger Smith."

A short pause. "I see," the woman said. "And this is regarding . . . ?"

"I'd like the opportunity to talk to Mr. Itzikoff about opportunities to provide counsel—"

"There is no Mr. Itzikoff. There is, however, a Ms. Itzikoff."

Sam gulped but pressed onward. "Could I speak to—"

"You are. And I appreciate you calling, Mr. Wentworth, but we're not in the market for new counsel."

"I understand, but if I could just get a moment of your time. Would you be free for lunch—"

"Please tell Robert hello for me. Thank you for your call." CLICK.

Sam stopped in midword. He hadn't been hung up on since—ever? And Robert? Who was Robert? Roger, not Robert. Did Roger even know this woman? He felt like the ground was slipping away underneath his feet and realized he'd been feeling that way an awful lot the last 24 hours. He'd been given another chance, and not only had he not closed new business with Universal Airlines, he hadn't even gotten a first meeting. Stupid, not checking if he was a she, not knowing the nature of Roger's relationship with her . . . stupid, stupid.

He reflexively grabbed at his stomach and flashed back to how as a high school quarterback he'd dreaded the feeling of being sacked. He had all too often been pummeled to the ground by defenders who penetrated the pocket, that small circle of protection supposedly created by Sam's teammates.

He never did have the best presence in the pocket. Too many times he lay sprawled with the breath squeezed out of him as if an elephant had belly flopped on a balloon.

The world felt very far away, and Sam decided he needed fresh air. He walked out of the office, taking care to steer clear of Roger, who had surely forgotten for the moment that Sam existed. Once out on the sidewalk, Sam knew there was only one place he could go.

"Welcome back, Sam!" Candace said, giving him a wink as she passed by en route to a table.

It was a small thing, the fact that she remembered his name, but Sam exhaled and smiled a touch. He knew he was falling for one of the oldest tricks in the sales book, but he fell anyway.

Sam collapsed into one of The Open Note's leather seats and waited for Candace to circle back. It didn't take long, and once again she had a chocolate chip cookie in hand.

"Day one of the new Sam didn't go so well, did it?"

"How can you tell?"

"Because it's not even 10 a.m. and you're already back in here."

Sam had to laugh at that one. "You're right." And he related the story of what had just happened—Candace winced in what appeared to be actual pain when told of the mistake in gender—and finished with, "I would just about kill for some more chocolate."

"Done," Candace said, getting to her feet. "And then you're going to do a little listening."

Again Sam watched her move through The Open Note. This time, though, he paid closer attention to the way she actually spoke to the customers. She got their names if they felt like giving them, and he could see her pause after each table, as if she was memorizing each name. And she was everywhere, attending to customers, watching over the register, checking the displays, stepping into the space beyond the tinted glass wall. What was back there anyway? He would ask her. But what he wanted to know first was how she managed to do every-thing in a way that was neither overbearing nor stress-inducing. Indeed, she looked like she knew exactly what she was doing every step of the way, and that impressed the heck out of Sam. She was Zen coffee shop lady.

"How do you do it?" Sam asked as Candace brought him a chocolate muffin. "How do you hold all this together?"

Candace smiled. "I'm glad you think this is together. You weren't here at eight this morning. That's a whole different story. I wouldn't have had time to string two sentences together."

"Still," Sam said, "you look calmer running around than I do when I'm asleep."

"Well, thank you, but trust me, that's a learned behavior," she replied. "It's really simple, actually. If you believe in who you are and what you do, the world opens wide to you."

"That's it?"

Candace smiled. "Of course that's not it. What do you think I am, a fortune cookie? Getting to this point takes a lot of work, but trust me, it's all so very worth it. Or at least I sure as heck hope it will be."

Sam took out his iPad. "Candace, I'm looking for pretty much any advice I can get at this point. How do you get customers? How do you hold on to customers?"

She bowed deeply. "You are about to get my Jedi training, young Sam," she said. "And the secret is . . ."

Sam typed "THE TRICK IS," then waited.

". . . there is no trick. Or at least no trickery or deception."

Sam looked up from his iPad. "No trick? Wait . . . what?"

"Put that down," she said, pointing to the iPad. "Just listen for a bit."

No secrets or trickery will get a genuine relationship started.
You've got to remember what regular human-to-human behavior
is like. Not salesperson-to-sucker manipulation.

"Start with the most basic elements of conversation. Think about this: What would happen if you went up to every person in this store and screamed a greeting at them?"

"You'd have the police in here in a hurry."

"Exactly. There's a time and a place for every kind of conversation, even a screaming one . . . though that's better saved for a stadium than a coffee shop. Now, suppose you had somebody who you knew was in need of legal services. Would you talk to them about, oh, coffee shops?"

"You need small talk, right?"

Candace made a knock-it-off face. "You know what I mean. If you're going to interest someone in what you have to offer, it has to be the right kind of interest, the right kind of conversation. Not to mention that it needs to be the right kind of person or you're wasting your time completely."

"What do you mean by—"

Candace held up a hand. "In a moment. Now, suppose you walked around to everyone you see out there on the street and introduced yourself. What's going to happen?"

"Lots of people turning their backs on me, at best."

"Exactly. What works at a cocktail party is a remarkably bad idea out on the street." She stood up again. "You've got to get back to work. But for now, think of it this way: right conversations, right people, right times, in the right way. That's how you do it."

"Seems easy enough."

"Then you're not listening very well. Sorry, Sam, but just because something seems simple doesn't mean it's easy. Remember how hard it was to learn how to drive?"

"I wrecked my father's car three days after I turned sixteen."

Candace winced again. "Hopefully we won't have anything that drastic happen here. But the point stands: driving is easy for you now, but there's a learning curve. And you get up and over that curve by doing it again and again."

"Right conversations, right people, right times, right way . . . got it," Sam said, committing it to memory.

"You don't need to believe me, Sam. I know you're a skeptic. Good advisors have to find the holes in situations and anticipate all the negative consequences. Kind of like a scientist. So here's what I ask: if you're so analytical, use the scientific method on what I'm telling you. Consider it a hypothesis, but you're not allowed to dismiss it out of hand unless you test it out—experiment with it—and prove it right or wrong," Candace said. She turned to make her rounds.

"Candace, wait," Sam said. "One more thing. What's on the other side of that glass wall? Through that door? Is that also the coffee shop?" He caught a glimpse of a funky-looking young woman carrying an oversized tray of scones and teacups through the door beyond the tinted glass. "Are you hosting tea time for the artists' guild over there or something?"

"What? Ha! No. That's The Open Note's coworking space. It's a shared working environment for people who think for a living; you know, people like you and other professionals and entrepreneurs and creative types. They want to have a place besides an office or a coffee shop to work and share ideas. They pay a monthly membership fee and the coffee and cookies are included, but they get much more than that. It is like a jambalaya of creativity in there. When you put a group of talented, like-minded people in close proximity in very cool surroundings, new relationships are bound to form, collaboration gets spontaneously conducted, ideas are sparked, businesses started, challenges overcome. Next time you come I'll take you on a tour."

"So let me get this straight . . . you're not just a cookie baker, and there's not a tea party in the other room?" Sam deadpanned.

Candace rolled her eyes and let out a sigh of mock exasperation.

THE RIGHT PLAY AT THE RIGHT TIME

6

Coach's Commentary

What does it mean to have the right conversations at the right times with the right people in the right contexts? Before we dissect what Sam did wrong on his call to Alex Itzikoff, let's start by figuring out what's right. *Right* has many meanings that matter in opening business relationships: (1) correct (as in "the right contact"), (2) brought into balance (as in "righted the ship"), (3) appropriate for the situation (as in "he said the right thing"), and (4) a privilege, benefit, or advantage (as in "he earned the right to meet with the CEO"). In the same way a quarterback must read the defense and call the right line-of-scrimmage audibles or a baseball batter must decide on the right pitches to chase, identifying what *right* means for you is situational and essential.

> In baseball, the right swing can take you far if it matches up with the right pitch. The batter, though, controls only one of those things.

George Brett, retired third baseman for the Kansas City Royals, hit 317 home runs in his career. All but five of them occurred, according to Brett, when he was not trying to hit a home run. They came because he focused on taking good swings and let the results take care of themselves. Former Atlanta Braves first baseman Fred McGriff belted 493 home runs during his professional baseball career. McGriff believes his home run success came from being on the receiving end of the right pitch—a specific one, thrown in just the right location that he hit for a home run—493 times. Similarly, in business development, we can control our approach to an encounter but we can't control the prospect's response. You do the right things the right way, and, you hope, you are matched up with a prospect who has the right appreciation for you and your skill set . . . and you knock it out of the park.

Like swinging a baseball bat the right way or progressing down the football gridiron with the right combination of plays, one thing that you need to get right is the order of operations: a set of things you do before and while you pursue prospects to ensure that you can stay in the game long enough to find the right client and opportunity.

Football coaches call this play sequencing. In our case, we're talking not about orchestrating a touchdown drive but about crafting an approach to opening a relationship with a prospect and keeping it open even after the prospect becomes a client. The ideal order of operations for opening business prospect relationships is as follows:

1. **Establish and articulate your claim to fame** (your Opening Strategy) before proceeding with your business development efforts. Who are you? What is it you do better than anyone else? Why should anyone care? Who—especially—should care about your unique genius? We'll help you figure that out in Chapters 7 and 8.

2. **Develop a prioritized prospect wish list.** Identify the top organizations and referral sources in your market that are most likely to be attracted by your positioning—not just who you most want as a client but, more important, who would find you most appealing. Specify the highest-probability prospects by name and also specify by name the executives in those companies with whom you need to build strong relationships. In baseball a manager can choose which

pitchers to bring in from the bullpen in certain situations, and in
business development you can pick which prospects you face.

3. **Activate your existing network of relationships.** Identify those
   individuals who are most willing and able to help you and find the
   ones who have an established relationship with the companies and
   people on your wish list. Make sure they know what you are famous
   for and the types of companies on your wish list. You're going to want
   their introductions and insights, but you first need to equip them to
   help you in the right way.

4. **Establish the content of value** that you will equip your referral
   relationships (in step 3) with to introduce you to the prospect
   in step 2. Content of value does *not* mean solicitation material.
   Anything that primarily benefits *you* is solicitation material:
   brochures, proposals, statements of qualifications, case studies, and
   so forth. Remember, you haven't yet earned the right to force your
   promotional materials on your prospect. Content of value *does* mean
   anything that is primarily of substantive benefit to your prospect:
   information, ideas, introductions, and so on. (We'll delve into this in
   the "connecting with content" discussion in Chapter 17.) You have
   to identify something of enough value that the prospect will want
   to meet with you. Prospects need to believe it is compellingly worth
   their while to carve time out of their insanely busy schedules to spend
   with you. Once you figure out what that value is, you can enlist your
   friends to make the right introduction.

5. **Prepare to improvise.** Sometimes the best-laid plans go awry,
   so, like a quarterback in a broken play, the best scorers are able to
   scramble and improvise a successful outcome to a play that doesn't
   go according to the formula. Sometimes you don't know anybody
   who can walk you in the door. Sometimes you can't figure out what
   content to bring. Sometimes you don't have time. Creative problem
   solving is an essential skill to hone in order to perform a proper

business development scramble. It can be taught in the same way that coaches develop and run quarterback scramble drills to prepare a player for game-time improvisation.

Let's compare this order of operations with the sequence that Sam followed in contacting Ms. Itzikoff.

Can Sam articulate what makes him uniquely valuable as an attorney? Does he know exactly which clients value his differences the most? Clearly not. What if he did know? He might have asked a few questions of Roger to determine whether Alex Itzikoff and Universal Airlines were likely to find Sam and his firm an attractive alternative to their current outside counsel.

Does Sam know who else might make a better prospect than Alex Itzikoff and Universal Airlines? No; he simply waits for Roger to tell him which prospects to approach. Do you really think that waiting for instructions from Roger is in Sam's best career interest? What would happen if instead Sam said, "Roger, I've been looking back at where I've delivered the most success for the firm and have a hypothesis about the prospects I ought to focus on for the best and quickest results. My clients of choice are especially . . . [Sam describes his ideal client and names a few prospects that fit the description]. What are your thoughts? I'm glad to contact Alex and appreciate the opportunity to do so. And I also would welcome your help on how I can build relationships with the ideal prospects I mentioned."

Let's take that a step further. Suppose Sam then said, "Roger, I noticed that you are on the same community nonprofit board of directors as [insert Sam's ideal prospect name here], who leads one of the companies on my client-of-choice wish list. Based on the research that I've done on that executive and his company, here's where our firm and my practice specifically may add value. [Sam would include his ideas about bringing substantive value here.] What do you think is the best way for me to approach [Sam's ideal prospect]?" With that approach, Sam is far more likely to get in front of more prospects who value his unique differences more often.

SECTION 2
OPENING STRATEGY

AVOID THE SCRUM

7

Roll Game Film

Roger Smith was turning the screw on the billable hour vise grip even as he expected more business development. The pressure to bill Habersham & Smith's clients for his time kept Sam buried in contracts, colleague meetings, and client discussions. It would be a couple days before Sam could get back to The Open Note, and during that time he spent many of his free moments going over Candace's mantra in his head, on his iPad, even in some old-fashioned handwritten notes. Right conversations . . . right time . . . right context . . . . It made plenty of sense in theory, but the more he thought about it, the more he realized it was like learning how to use the gas and brakes on a car already in motion.

He knew how to converse, of course; one doesn't get through college and law school without at least some measure of ability to start, carry, and, if necessary, gracefully exit a conversation. But he was starting to realize that there was an art to a conversation with a business end, a natural flow that wasn't actually the scripted performance he'd thought it was.

He brought this up to Candace the next time he stopped by The Open Note, and she paused. "Give me a second," she said. "I want to figure out how best to answer this."

While he waited, Sam scrolled through his list of potential contacts and realized that for each one, he had almost no recollection of how he'd gotten the name, no mental connection other than "someone gave this to me." That, he understood, simply wouldn't do any longer. He needed to know more. No more "Mr. or Ms.?" mistakes.

"I've got it," Candace said, returning to his table. "Stand up."

Sam did, then made an at-your-service flourish.

"Want more coffee?" Candace asked.

Sam looked at his nearly empty cup. "Sure, that'd be great."

"All right," Candace said, motioning toward the five-person line snaking back from the register. "Go wait in line."

Sam, a touch perplexed, began to walk toward the end of the line, but Candace grabbed him. "Sam. Come on. You're going to just go along with everyone else?"

"It seemed the polite thing to do."

Candace pointed to herself. "Hello. Owner right here. I can go behind the counter and get you what you need, you know."

"I thought it would be rude."

Candace gently smacked him on the arm. "Working with your friends isn't rude, Sam. You've been a good customer for a couple of weeks now. You're entitled to some extra privileges . . . if you think about asking for them."

Sam paused for a moment, then smiled. "Well, then, Candace, since you're offering," he said, extending his cup, "how about a refill? Please."

"By all means." She filled his cup and then returned. "Don't get used to that. I was making a point."

"Wouldn't dream of it," Sam said.

"The point, Sam, is this: you can take the path that everyone else travels, and you can get in line with everyone else. Or you can look to find new options, new routes, new ways to get to where you want. And the easiest routes are those lined with people who already know you, like you, and trust you: your friends. You can't avoid asking and benefiting from their help. These days, you have to."

Sam looked around. This was a coffee shop, yes, but it also had the feel of a family room. Board games, musical instruments, the art on the walls; you could get yourself a cup of joe if you wanted, but you could get so much more as well. Candace had sidestepped the Starbucks and Caribous of the world to create something at once both familiar and new. It was a place where you felt you were always among friends.

The minute anyone walked through the front door of The Open Note, he or she could see that this place had a feel different from that of the chain coffee shops. It was far more than that. He wasn't sure it was really a coffee shop at all, in fact. Earlier, Candace had kept her promise to take him on a tour of the mysterious space on the other side of the glass wall. It was different, all right.

The glass door opened into a broad common area with wide-planked wooden floors, wooden tables, an indoor tree, a glowing fireplace, and soft, energy-sensible lighting from what seemed an impossibly high ceiling. It was a beehive abuzz. But it was a hive that balanced privacy and collaboration. There were glass-enclosed offices along one wall, and another set of open workspaces lined the windows overlooking the street outside. There were conference rooms stocked with so much technology that they could have been Space Shuttle cockpits, and there were seating areas where you could sink into a brown leather body glove of a chair with your laptop. The cozy communal Open Note had broken down everything stuffy about the typical office and swapped it for couches, colorful walls, and fine-art photography and folk art by local artists.

Sam thought he recognized the blue blazer and jeans guy and the funky girl he had seen before slipping in and out of the café. They were chatting near a rough-hewn set of shelves in the corner that hosted a lending library of books on entrepreneurship, collaboration, innovation, and design. The two of them looked like they wouldn't be very comfortable in the formal, blue blood atmosphere of Habersham & Smith.

"Here we have members, clients, and colleagues, not customers," Candace declared. "The members here are all rising professionals or entrepreneurial leaders, and all of them are thinkers, makers, and doers," she continued. "Many of them are part of organizations with their own office space, but they and their colleagues use this as an adjunct home away from home." Candace described an affordable menu of membership options, ranging from $125 a month to $450 a month for unlimited, 24/7 key card access to the space. There weren't any binding contracts. Members paid on a month-to-month basis so that they wouldn't be stuck with a contract if their situations changed sometime down the line.

"The open gallery is perfect for hosting thought leadership events, networking get-togethers, or happy hours," Candace told him. "Members can attend a weekly breakfast speakers series and lunch-n-learns and receive referrals for a variety of services from bookkeeping to marketing. We also get them discounts for online business tools and to local business resources: restaurants, the sports club next door, Zipcar, and office supply stores. And, of course," Candace added, "members get a selection of items from our café included in their membership fee. Questions?"

Questions? Sam had more questions than a jamboree of *Jeopardy* contestants. His most pressing question, though, was, How had Candace gotten from a standing start to where she was now? He was impressed with what she had created and meant to ask his question in a flattering way, but the litigator in him pressed on. "No offense, Candace," Sam said, "but 'do something different' is kind of straightforward, isn't it? There's nothing different under the sun. Just variations on a theme. So you're not only competing with Starbucks but with Regus executive suites and the office building next door, right?"

Candace answered his interrogation with a question of her own. "What separates you from everybody else trying for the same client, the same job, the same goal you are?"

"Well, there's . . ." Sam paused. "Hmm."

"Tricky question, isn't it? Your mother knows what makes you special. Nobody else does. And sorry to say this, but nobody else cares about you as much as your mother does. So, Sam, tell me: Who are you? Where did you come from? What makes you a special and unique flower?"

"What is this? A Barbara Walters interview?" Sam laughed, but Candace met his retort with a warm smile. So Sam talked about himself, talked in a way he hadn't in years, if ever. He started with the basics: good solid family upbringing, Little League baseball and Scouts and church and the whole good-childhood swing. He got good grades in high school and parlayed them into admission to a strong college. Fraternity life, football on the weekends, a serious girlfriend. And then, nearing the end of his junior year, he realized he wasn't quite sure what to do with his life.

So he punted. He applied to law school.

Much to his surprise, he received several acceptances. His grades were, like so much else in his life, decent but not spectacular. He ended up at a decent but not spectacular law school, where he pursued three years of a decent but not spectacular academic career. And when he was done, when he'd received both his diploma and a solid job offer, he had an accomplishment in which he could take some pride.

"No offense, Sam," Candace said, turning his words back on him, "but that story sounds an awful lot like a hundred others I've heard."

"I know," Sam said, nodding his head.

"Wait! No! Don't get down! I wasn't trying to say anything bad!" Candace said, waving her hands. "All I meant was that you've got a pretty straight-forward backstory. And that's no problem at all. What you've got to do is figure out what you have to offer going forward. Why should anyone select you as a legal advisor instead of someone else? What makes you unique? Besides an unhealthy addiction to chocolate, apparently."

Sam pushed aside the muffin. "Duly noted," he said. "Where do I even start to figure that out?"

"Start right where you are. With what you have. Right here and now," Candace said.

"But here's what's obvious: taking the path that everyone else is on is the best way to get either hung up waiting or stepped on by others. Playing the same role in the same way as all of your peers and partners and pursuing business using the same approaches—that is to say, very blandly and old school—may feel like it's the commonsense path, the one that will allow you to coast with the least resistance. But it's not necessarily the one that will accelerate your professional standing. And it may not be the one that will make you happy."

Sam thought about it for a moment, and then he shook his head. "*Happy* is a word I know but not necessarily a feeling I experience all that much. Someone once described happiness as the good sensation you get when you consider someone else's lousy situation," Sam said, attempting to deflect the uncomfortable issue with his trademark dark humor. Candace didn't laugh. Sam kept stumbling. "Really, I don't know. I guess you accrue experience, you try your best to pile up more good times than bad, and that's how you reach happiness. But going too far off the beaten path sounds like a painful trip to me."

Candace gave him a mock-angry scowl. "Really? You really believe that?"

"There's a reason the well-trodden path is the well-trodden path. It's worked for lots of people for a long time."

Candace waved her hand in a way that took in the entire café, coworking space and all. "Seriously? What generation are you actually from? Look around. Everybody's on a phone, on a tablet, on a laptop. This is a whole new world. What worked before may not work now, and what works now may not have worked then."

Sam nodded. "I know; I get that. Disruption and innovation and all of that. But still, there are some standards, some methods of business that are always going to work."

"Like the way your hero, Roger Smith, handles things right?" Candace stood and held up a finger. "Hold on just a second." She walked behind the counter, grabbed a coffeepot and a cup and saucer, and returned to Sam's table. She put the cup down and without waiting began to pour coffee. The cup filled up, up, up . . . up to the brim and then over the edge of the brim. Surface tension held the coffee at the very verge of spilling.

"Now," Candace said, "drink up."

"Wait a second," Sam said. "The cup's so full, it's going to spill if I even touch it."

"Exactly," Candace said.

"The cup is your skull. The coffee is the old thoughts that are
filling your head. There's no room in there for anything new.
You've got to clear your mind of all the old biases and
expectations, Sam. It's a new day."

Sam sat back. "Fine. You and the coffee have convinced me. What do I
need to do to think outside the cup?"

"Start thinking about your head as a cup, for instance. Or as a manila
folder. Or a potted plant. Or whatever. Think creatively. Think strangely. And
think highly of yourself."

"But why? We just discussed how I don't have much to offer."

"You have everything to offer. You are the only Sam Wentworth there is.
You've got a distinct combination of experiences, knowledge, skills, and per-
spectives that no one else in the world shares. It's up to you to figure out how
to package those assets in a way that brings significant value to just the right
folks and that's distinct from anyone else at the party. Where is it that you can
have a monopoly? I don't mean the game Monopoly; I mean no competitors.
For what clients are you the only real game in town? And I'll stop you before
you go down Cynical Street again—the answer isn't nobody.'"

"Fair enough," Sam said. "So how about you? Besides coffee, cookies, and
a place to get free Wi-Fi and some office space, what do you really offer that's
different from anyone else?"

Candace looked around, taking it all in. The café had gotten through the
midmorning rush and was now in the short lull before lunchtime. Here and
there, customers were sipping their drinks, some chatting, some in their own
world focused on their phones or tablets. But Sam noticed that they were all
extremely comfortable, at ease, and relaxed in a way that most professionals
definitely weren't at this time of the morning. A murmur of productivity per-
meated the coworking spaces, too.

"Community," Candace said. "That's what I try to promote. A real,
working *collaborative* community."

She pointed down the street at the Starbucks. "There was no way on earth I was going to compete with them. Running up against them would be like running straight into an NFL defense with no pads on. And Sam, I hardly compete with traditional office space providers. I gave you the full tour. Can you tell me truthfully that the offices you've seen in your career really look like this?"

"So how did you do it?"

"Realistically, assuming you actually want to play the game, you've only got three options when it comes to your competition: you go through them, you go over them, or you go around them." She ticked off the options on her fingers. "I didn't have the money to go over Starbucks or the average office real estate tycoon. I'm not sure anybody this side of Mark Zuckerberg does. And obviously I couldn't go through them. So that leaves around. Figure out where they come up short and outrun them around the edge."

Sam nodded. "Makes sense."

"Here's the thing. Most coffee shops are now in the business of promoting a false kind of community. They want you to believe that you're part of the family, but they undercut that with their actions. They remove outlets, they make the chairs hard and uncomfortable, they take down bulletin boards for community involvement and replace them with anonymous works of mass-produced art. It's profitable, but does it have warmth? And then there are the giant corporations trying to slap a coat of collaborative, innovative paint on their massive bureaucracies by designating some spaces with beanbag chairs, a foosball table, and a do-it-yourself espresso machine. Too often that redecoration activity isn't matched by a behavior change in the leadership, so there's still no real space on-site to break from the cycle of internal competition and rigid thinking. Besides, who wants to work out of a beanbag chair?"

"It's comfortable, I guess."

"But you know what it lacks, Sam?" Candace leaned forward and pointed a coffee stirrer right at him. "It lacks authenticity. And people know inauthenticity when they see it."

Over the speakers, gentle acoustic music began cascading. Sam's first instinct was to scowl in frustration, but as he listened—really listened—he started to unwind. Cascading notes and chords blanketed the café, and Sam allowed himself to begin relaxing.

"Building a community and fostering collaboration is a tricky business, but it's one that pays off in the long term," Candace continued, smiling at the music. "And it's not just about coffee and snacks. That's the cost of doing business."

It was a seductive pitch, Sam had to admit. The community here, the sense of belonging, of being a part of something more than oneself . . . that was a rare feeling indeed in the city, and Sam realized that Candace had stumbled onto—or, perhaps more accurately, had scoped out—an opportunity to grow herself in a way that had eluded her larger, more lumbering competitors.

"You're going to hear me say this once, Sam, and then you won't hear it again," Candace said. "The way you'll get the most from The Open Note is this: if you do it right, if you come here with the right mindset—open, listening, broadening—you will be more successful in everything you do. I don't guarantee it, but I've got a pretty good track record so far."

Sam nodded. He could see it. And he could believe it.

Candace stood up. "I'm on the road visiting my other Open Notes next week. We connect regularly on Skype, but nothing beats face to face; besides, I've got other Sams in other lands to help," Candace said. "I've got to get some things together, but I'll see you tomorrow."

This time, Sam noticed, it wasn't a question.

OWN THE OPEN FIELD

8

Coach's Commentary

Candace knows that running headlong at her competition is a great way to get crushed. She's carefully crafted The Open Note to stand apart from its competitors.

She started with her customers of choice. It wasn't hard. She wanted to work with people who were like her, people driven to create or add something of meaningful value to the world. A few years earlier she had read a book by a guy named Richard Florida called *The Rise of the Creative Class*. These were people in big-thinking jobs such as scientists, architects and engineers, marketing and new media entrepreneurs, poets and artists, heath industry leaders, strategy consultants, and other big-intellect advisory professionals and others who get hired for their brainpower and creative problem-solving skills. Like Candace, creative class professionals didn't like being confined to a traditional office with traditional boundaries. They craved freedom and flexibility. They wanted to dress comfortably and set their own hours. Sometimes they needed solitude. Sometimes they needed collegiality. Either way, they demanded the right to choose when, where, and how they activated their intellects for optimal benefit. Coffee shops and coworking spaces were busting at the seams because of the rapid growth of this workforce sector.

Candace saw increasingly high-decibel, mega-chain coffee cafés waging a silent war against what they considered to be laptop-wielding freeloaders camping out in their best seats for hours nursing one cup of java. In effect, Candace asked, "What if the customers that the giant coffee chains view as hobos I view as enterprising knowledge workers looking for an alternative space to create businesses?"

She, in contrast, saw coworking spaces as a hypergrowth trend. These were the informal but well-equipped shared working environments in which the creative class could congregate to get work done and collaborate with like-minded entrepreneurial executives. Coworking spaces made money through membership dues and additional service fees. They were terrific spots for business events, training, meetings, and thought work where you could feel safe leaving your laptop to get a cup of coffee. Only thing was, Candace noticed that the free communal food and drink provided in those environments was sorely lacking; she believed that the more seasoned, higher-income coworkers would pay for more and better.

Candace believed, too, that she could use her foodie sensibility and unique skills to orchestrate great customer experiences and connect people to better serve her unique market. She asked, "What if a coworking space could have the food amenities of a gourmet café without giving up a stimulating work environment where great intentional connections could be made?"

At the intersection of those questions, Candace discovered her hybrid solution. The Open Note space was deliberately crafted to be both a café and a coworking space where creative class executives are encouraged to spend more time, not less. Attracted first by the quality of the café's food and environment, select patrons are given a glimpse of the coworking experience and gently enticed to shift from an occasional café visitor to a regular coworking space member. The businesspeople and entrepreneurs who step into The Open Note not only get a tasty treat for their money, they get a creativity spark and business-networking boost. Candace's ultimate mission became no less than changing the way people live, think, connect, and earn a living.

A great running back uses his agility and vision to find the open hole, sometimes even before it develops, and sprint through to the resulting open field, untouched like a thoroughbred. In the same way, Candace had broken through.

Now she's provoking Sam to do the same with his business development efforts: to find the open field. In American football and soccer, playing in open space means getting into field position devoid of defenders, particularly between the ball and the goal. On the soccer field, intentional movement and positioning by a team on one part of the pitch can open up an area free of competitors on another part where a pass to an open teammate can lead to a shot on goal. We call that intentional, practiced set of activities— the approach that Candace used to position The Open Note to win—an Opening Strategy.

An Opening Strategy is your description of what's right for your positioning and development efforts. The opposite of an Opening Strategy is visible from the sidelines of a children's soccer game: a cluster of eight-year-olds converging on the ball, leaving no one open to receive a pass and no one in control. Let's call this random clustering of competitors around a scarce, desirable object a chaotic mess, although most of us can come up with a more colorful term or two.

In business development, your Opening Strategy is how you define your open field—your claim to fame. It's how you avoid a chaotic mess and professional obscurity.

To create a successful Opening Strategy, you need to describe four main components:

1. **Clients.** Who are your clients of choice?

2. **Capabilities.** What is it you do, and what are the biggest benefits you deliver to those clients?

3. **Competitors.** How is it that you provide a far superior result than your competitors can?

4. **Consequences.** What's the payoff for your client and for you from your great work?

For your Opening Strategy to be useful, your descriptions of these components must be very specific. Many professionals are afraid of being defined too narrowly. They want to stay open to receiving work from anyone who will pay them, and in so doing, they misunderstand the intention of an Opening Strategy.

An Opening Strategy doesn't require that you be *exclusively* specialized in only one thing. It does require that you be *especially* great at something, though.

An Opening Strategy is not an attempt to get you to eliminate any aspect of your practice. It is a direct attempt to get you to *emphasize* something. Because *you* are the main tool to execute your marketing effort and because *you* have limited time, energy, and financial support, you need to choose the audiences and activities with which you are most likely to succeed with the least effort. Your Opening Strategy guides you to the activities that will *raise the odds that you can open the door of a prospect* and convert that prospect to a strong client. That's not going to happen if you promote yourself as serving everyone and anyone in anything and everything they need done. It's not believable, not distinctive, and not memorable for prospects, colleagues, or referral sources. As you go through this series of exercises to define your Opening Strategy, push yourself beyond mundane, generic responses.

Let's drill deeper, starting with your preferred clients.

Who are your clients of choice? If you could pick just one type of client to work with, how would you describe that client? Consider both the company and the key client contact with which you would work. For what company and executive are you *the* provider or advisor of choice? Paint a vivid picture of your ideal clients by describing them on four "S" dimensions: their statistics, similarities, situation, and suitability.

1. **Statistics.** Describe your ideal clients by the objective and quantifiable aspects of their business. For instance:

    - *Industry.* What's their specific field of business? What product or service do they provide?

    - *Size.* How much annual revenue and how many employees do they have?

    - *Market share.* Are they a leader, runner-up, or a distant follower?

    - *Location.* Where are they located?

    - *Customers.* Are they primarily serving businesses or consumers?

    - *Decision makers.* Who within your ideal client is the typical decision maker? What is that person's title and function? How old is that person? How was he or she educated? How is that person being held accountable? How is that person rewarded? To whom does he or she report?

    - *Buying criteria.* What buying criteria *does* your ideal prospect use to choose firms like yours and a professional like you? What criteria *should* they use instead or in addition?

2. **Similarities.** Describe the ideal client by attributes relating to his or her background, values, attitudes, or cultural style and its similarity to you, your firm, and the clients you are especially great at serving.

- *Affinity.* Consider the key individuals at your ideal client. What do you and your best clients typically have in common? Did you go to the same college? Grow up in the same hometown? Work at the same prior employer? Share the same hobby? Have kids the same age or in the same circumstances?

- *Culture.* How do their company's culture and values match yours and your firm's?

- *Growth.* Has your ideal client been experiencing high growth, sustainable growth, or slow growth?

- *Structure and funding.* How is your ideal client legally structured and organized? Is it a corporation, S corp., LLC, LLP, PC, franchisor, franchisee, joint venture, spin-off, family-run? Is it centralized? Decentralized? Global, regional, local, virtual? How has it been funded? IPO? Bank debt? Angel investor? Bootstrapped? Private equity? Venture capital? Friends? Family?

- *Goals.* What are the top strategic objectives of the organization and its leadership? What are the top strategic objectives of the key decision maker for your services? What motivates them? What concerns them? What roadblocks stand in their way? What has been this individual's past interaction, success, or failure working with professionals like you?

- *Connections.* Do you have a common contact that can warm up the relationship and instantly anoint you with a high degree of credibility?

3. **Situation.** What tectonic shift is taking place in the company that enables you to deliver unique high-value solutions? What problem do they need to have solved?

- *Transitions.* Merger, sale, restructuring, initial public offering, going private, spinning out, management changes?

- *Aspirations.* In what ways would your ideal clients expect to be different and better when your potential engagement is complete? Where do they see their company or industry or their own careers or economic circumstances in one to five years?

- *Compliance.* What must they get done to avoid running afoul of legal or governmental requirements?

4. **Suitability.** How attractive are you to the prospects? Why is it that they will find you to be a more appropriate advisor than your competitors? Whether you are especially interested in a prospect matters less than whether the prospect is likely to be interested in you and your firm.

For best results, use all of the four S approaches to create a vivid and specific description of your ideal prospective client. Begin with the situation your ideal client faces that you are best at addressing. End with the statistics of companies for which you have unique knowledge and experience. "You know, when a company makes an acquisition, how hard it is to integrate the new team— especially when the company is a family-owned business in, say, the textile industry, where loyalties run deep?" If you are clearly attractive to the prospect and you have a common contact, move it farther up your prospect wish list.

CAPABILITIES

Capabilities are the elements that clients purchase when they hire a professional advisor or engage a business services firm. Capabilities include *what* a professional does, *how* she does it, and what it *feels* like to work with her. The sum of these factors is the total benefit provided to a client from his association with a particular firm, and so capabilities are best described as the payoff, benefit, or value that your best client realizes from working with you.

1. **What do you do?** There are two ways to answer this. The first is to provide a literal and internally focused view of your practice or

business. What are your specific technical skills and competencies? In what area are you a significant expert? What client problem are you most adept as solving? How and in what *one main way* do you provide the most benefit and value to clients? This is useful but limiting. Candace is in the restaurant business. She sells coffee and doughnuts. Really, that's it? That's what she's about?

The second approach requires a lateral and client-focused perspective. Consider the reframing approach recommended by the Harvard Business School professor Theodore Levitt. In his famous 1960 *Harvard Business Review* article "Marketing Myopia," Levitt attributed the failure of many major railroad companies to their continuing to act as if they were in the railroad business in the face of rising competition from cars, trucks, and airlines. Had they considered sooner that they were in the transportation business, or the logistics business, or the vacation experience business, they might have made bolder moves to avoid commoditization and stemmed their market share decline.

Years later and in a completely different market, Starbucks decided it was not as much in the business of selling cups of coffee as it was in the field of providing a "coffee culture experience." Candace has taken that to a new level. She's transforming her customers through community and connection and, oh, by the way, some spectacular coffee and cookies.

See if you can reframe the category of service you provide (or the business you're in) in a compelling way that describes the true benefit you deliver.

---

2. **How do you do it?** What service quality do you demonstrate, and how do you apply your expertise? Are you especially fast and accurate? Or are you thorough and persistent? Or are you an incredible listener

who can absorb a mind-numbing set of facts and translate them into a concise, usable answer? Or do you have some other unique traits that make you especially valuable as a professional?

Hint: Avoid mundane descriptions such as "I'm responsive" or "I'm very experienced." So what? Everyone says that. "Oh, but I really am," you protest. Everyone else says that too. *Show* it; don't *tell* it. Do you have a proprietary process that guarantees results? Can you point to success metrics from prior engagements? Is there something in your background that demonstrates unimpeachable evidence of your prowess? *Put it out there*. If there is not, either get some or rethink what you do best.

3. **How does it feel?** Because it is often the hardest for analytical professionals like us to appreciate, we'll start with how it feels to work as a professional like, say, you, Sam, or me. Think about products. Do you prefer your coffee from Starbucks or Dunkin' Donuts? Assuming that both serve a tasty cup o' joe, it feels different to go through the Starbucks experience as opposed to the Dunkin' Donuts one. This may all sound soft to you, but test it out for yourself. Consider what you've bought in the past and why. Often, it is the emotional "feel" you prefer that sways you one way or another. The same thing happens with professionals. We get hired for our competence, sure, but also for our likability and fit with the client's personal style or corporate culture and situational imperative.

Activities

* Consider what it feels like to work with certain professionals. Litigators, for instance, come in a couple of flavors. One type is the belligerent fighter who will berate and intimidate the other side into capitulation. The other type is the calm, cool diplomat who will guide the other side into an agreeable arrangement. Is one approach better than the other? It depends on the clients and their issues as well as their preferences.

- What does it feel like for the client to work with you? Calming or energizing? Does it feel to the client like she has a bulldog on her side? Or does it feel like she has a wise and even-keeled counselor? No one style is better than another, but recognizing which style a professional brings to his engagements helps everyone better articulate that professional's significant competitive difference.

- Just for fun, see if you can find an evocative phrase to describe what it feels like for a client to work with you, a phrase that sparks emotions and imagery and accurately though metaphorically describes your unique capabilities: "I am their *success partner*" or "I am their *legal quarterback*" or "I am their *insurance policy* to make sure things work out right" or "I am their whisper in the ear, *behind the curtains confidant*" or "I am the *stabilizing mechanism*" or "I'm like a *Green Beret* who swoops in first" or "I'm like an intelligence operative who unearths the real facts of the situation." Or _____ [fill in the blank].

In pro football, players are often nicknamed for what it feels like to play against them. Check out these football players' nicknames as a stimulus to come up with evocative descriptors that fit what it feels like to work with you.

"Sweetness." The late Walter Payton's defining characteristic was his smooth running style, which propelled him into the Hall of Fame and served as the centerpiece of one of the greatest teams of all time, the 1985 Chicago Bears.

William "Refrigerator" Perry. Going up against the 335-pound defensive lineman, a teammate of Payton's, felt like trying to block a moving kitchen appliance.

Mean Joe Green. This Pittsburgh Steelers defenseman didn't earn his moniker through his sweet game time demeanor.

Too Tall Jones. The six-foot nine-inch Dallas Cowboys star swatted away so many opposing team passes that the NFL started tracking a "pass deflection" statistic. How about throwing a ball through the giant arms of that guy?

Megatron. Detroit Lions wide receiver Calvin Johnson is a certain future Hall of Famer and one of the best ever to play his position. He carries the menacing nickname of the villain from the *Transformers* movies even though he's as calm as they come in real life.

Machine Gun Kelly. Buffalo Bills quarterback Jim Kelly was famous for his rapid-fire no-huddle offense, which left little time for the opposing team to figure out how to defend.

Joe Cool. Joe Montana led the San Francisco 49ers to four Super Bowl victories. But it was his ability to remain calm in tough comeback situations that earned his title and unnerved competitors.

Matty Ice. Atlanta Falcons quarterback Matt Ryan, like Joe Cool before him, gained his nickname because of his ice-in-the-veins approach to pulling out a last-minute touchdown drive to win the game.

COMPETITORS

Great client cultivators and rainmakers can describe their key competitors so that they can uniquely position their offering away from those of other services firms. Your competitor assessment should consider these factors:

- **Attributes.** Describe the client and capability dimensions on which you most and least favorably compare with your competitor firms.

    - Who are your most direct competitors, and how do you compare?

    - What one competitor or colleague would you most want to be compared to? What specific attributes of that competitor or colleague do you most admire? How does he or she develop business?

- What one competitor or colleague would you hate to be compared to? What specific attributes of that competitor or colleague do you most want to avoid having?

- Who are your competitors' ideal clients? Why?

- On what benefits and attributes do your competitors typically compete?

- **Substitutes.** Describe the services that address the same client matters you do but do so with an alternative approach. To solve a particular problem, for instance, a client can hire you or a competitor or could solve it by using internal resources or hiring a staffing company to provide supplemental resources. Technological solutions are increasingly displacing professional services firms for a range of client issues. Where a client might have previously hired a recruiter to search for a very specific type of talent, the client might now choose to do it in-house by using LinkedIn or similar online tools.

  - Name the substitute solutions that can undermine your success.

  - Describe the situations in which these threats are most likely to arise.

  - Articulate how and/or why your solution is far superior to the substitute.

- **Absolutes.** Describe the situations in which you win hands down every time.

  - Why and when do prospects seek you out and/or sole source you?

  - In what circumstances do your prospects not even consider certain competitors?

CONSEQUENCES

Ultimately, we get hired and rehired for the consequences or results we produce. How do your clients become better off for having chosen you? Both the tangible and the intangible benefits received by your client are important to articulate.

Further, we are motivated to serve our prospects and clients again and again because of the consequences or results we produce. Why do you do what you do? What is it about the process and results related to what you do that gets you most enthused? What is most gratifying about your work? Enthusiasm makes you more likable to a prospect who needs a driven success partner on her or his team.

Your prospects' belief and trust in you are enhanced by the passion you show for your professional mission. You don't have to fake inspiration if you are truly motivated by a compelling "why?"

Your "why?" might be an internal motivator: "I'm very intellectually competitive and just get huge enjoyment out of unraveling problems that others find intractable." It could be an external motivator such as seeing others succeed: "When a client tells me that our work together has changed his or her life, it makes it all worthwhile." It could be an altruistic motivation: "My efforts to help clients lead directly to a cleaner, healthier environment." It could be an acquisitive motivation: "I love it when my interests are aligned with my client—when I help you make a lot more money, I make a lot more money too." Any of these is fine as long as you've dug deep and are able to articulate something meaningful and true.

Criteria for a Successful Opening Strategy

✓ Attractive enough to lure more of the right prospects more often

✓ Simple and inspiring enough for you to describe with passion

✓ Specific enough that you can build a focused prospect list

✓ Broad enough that you have a sufficient pool of prospects

✓ Situation-focused enough to let you initially penetrate, then expand

✓ Financially grounded enough for maximum profit potential

PUTTING IT TOGETHER

The most useful way to craft your Opening Strategy is in story form: your Opening Story. Done right, your Opening Story serves as your internal guide to how you spend your business development time and resources, as a formal positioning statement should. But it also allows you to talk about it to other people who aren't marketing MBAs and make them understand. Your Opening Story is not as academic as a positioning statement, nor is it as glib and sales-slick as an elevator pitch. It is an engaging conversational way to illustrate your claim to fame. The point isn't to tell a story that wins a 100 percent share of your prospect's professional services wallet. It is to tell a true and compelling story that opens initial conversations, continued dialogue, and first engagements with just the right prospects.

Opening Story Format

You know how _____ (kind of client with which you excel) sometimes _____ (describe the specific difficult problem where you are of most help) and as a result (describe the negative consequence to your client of not solving the problem effectively)? That's exactly the type of situation where I can help in a way my competitors can't because _____ (describe the capabilities that differentiate you). Because of this, my clients experience _____ (describe the soft benefits your clients enjoy because they chose you) and they see specific results that look like this _____ (provide hard, quantitative examples proving your efficacy). That's why I do what I do; I love helping clients experience _____ (those benefits and results) and to see the changes in their lives and business that follow.

You don't have to make your words fit this format precisely, but try to make it work at least directionally. Don't sweat it; crummy first drafts are the best starting point. You can refine and iterate from there. Good stories have clear characters, compelling settings, dramatic conflicts, and heroes with superpowers. Your Opening Story should too.

For example, what if Sam crafted his story to reflect his interest in the same market Candace serves? He might tell his story in this way:

"You know how the leaders of fast-growth social enterprises and creative class companies—like technology ventures with a world-changing mission—sometimes prioritize opportunity ahead of risk and as a result can make hasty decisions—like failing to include certain legal terms for fear of screwing up a deal? That's exactly the type of situation where I can help in a way my competitors can't because having grown up in a family of serial entrepreneurs, I've learned how to navigate risk in a way that accelerates growth rather than impeding it and I've felt the pain of mismanaging that balance. Because of this, my clients experience an attorney who keeps them safe and growing at the same time—meeting risk roadblocks with creative problem-solving skills that produce a "how else?" alternative solution. I act as an outside general counsel and consigliere for early-stage ventures, helping them raise growth funds, negotiate smarter customer agreements, and ensure solid employee agreements. That leads to specific results that look like this: last week I helped a biomedical company close its first round of venture capital, which will allow it to test a new chronic disease medication. That's why I do what I do, I love helping clients experience the freedom to create products and services that can massively improve the world and to see the changes in their lives and business that follow."

TESTING YOUR OPENING STRATEGY

You can tell if your Opening Strategy is unique, useful, and specific enough if it helps you decide how and with whom to most effectively spend your time, energy, and financial resources. Here are some ways to test your Opening Strategy:

1. Gather a list of 10 or 20 companies and identify the three or four you would target first based on your Opening Strategy and Opening Story. Does it help? If not, go back to the Opening Strategy drawing board.

2. If certain prospects have already been assigned to you, use your Opening Strategy to prioritize the executives and issues at the prospect that you are best equipped to serve first.

3. Ask your closest contacts or colleagues to describe what they think you're famous for. If they can't do it or come nowhere close to describing your Opening Strategy, try sharing your proposed story with them. Do they get it? Does it strike true for them? Do they act on it by providing prospective clients or referral sources based on your description?

4. Can you eliminate certain activities that you had considered marketing but that really don't support, reinforce, or draw strength from your Opening Strategy? Can you readily conceive of other activities, thought leadership ideas, and relationships that fit better?

Your Opening Strategy and Opening Story are guideposts to determine what is right in your business development efforts. They determine how you spend your time, with whom you spend, it and what you discuss. Your strategy and story determine how you present yourself, where, and when. In short, they determine the connections, conversations, and context that are most likely to help you win more often.

Bring Your Opening Strategy to Life

- **Do not manage to the exceptions.** "Special cases" and "Well, yeah, but in this situation it doesn't apply" will kill you. Remember, your Opening Strategy isn't about what you exclusively do; it's what you especially do, what you prioritize. Do not dilute and do not permit your team to dilute the positioning by constant concern with exceptions and fear of excluding something.

- **Everything reflects strategy.** Ensure that all your client-facing activities and materials are informed by your Opening Strategy, from your LinkedIn Profile to your proposals and right down to the granular such as billing statement messages.

- **Make strategy-centered decisions.** Vigilantly use your Opening Strategy as a decision tool for spending your business development time and money. Does it reflect and reinforce your strategy? No? Don't do it.

- **Tell the story again and again.** Consistently practice translating your Opening Strategy into conversational messaging that goes beyond technical details and ascends to the level of business discussion.

- **Proactively pursue specific prospects.** Use the strategy to intentionally select, prioritize, and pursue the most potentially profitable prospects. That means moving well beyond prospects you stumble upon unintentionally. It means directing your referral sources to focus on referrals that better fit your Opening Strategy.

Before we move into the next section, here's a visual summary of the elements you need to build a useful Opening Strategy.

01 *Right Opening Strategy*

- **CLIENTS**
  - Statistics
  - Similarities
  - Situations
  - Suitability

- **CAPABILITIES**
  - What You Do
  - How You Do It
  - How It Feels to Work with You

- **COMPETITORS**
  - Attributes
  - Substitutes
  - Absolutes

- **CONSEQUENCES**
  - Client Payoff
  - Your "Why?"

SECTION 3
RIGHT CONNECTIONS: THE RELATIONSHIP ADVANTAGE

THE TRIPLE OPTION PLAY

9

Roll Game Film

Sam had never been a master networker, though he knew how to play the game, of course. Everybody who had any kind of success in college and law school knew the routine. You had to spot the leading lights early, work your way into their orbit, and create your own little solar system along the way. Learn names, colleges, and hometowns; keep a list of relatively inoffensive small-talk topics at the ready; keep an eye out for some possible shared experiences in class or at a party for bridge building and bonding.

He knew that networking was a necessary element of his career advancement, a way for him to break out of constant reliance on senior partners for contacts and leads. Still, for Sam, trying to learn networking was like trying to make a right turn onto an interstate; he didn't know where to find an opening or how to get up to speed fast enough.

He'd tried; oh, how he'd tried. Not long before, he'd played golf with an old law school buddy, and somewhere on the back nine the talk had turned to business . . . or the lack thereof. He'd mentioned, casually but not casually, that he'd like an introduction to his buddy's chief financial officer and, well, he got one.

The introduction came in the form of a poorly written e-mail, so stiff and creaky that it could have been a form letter, introducing Sam as "a pal of mine your going to be impressed with," grammatical error and all. Not surprisingly, Sam didn't get a call from the CFO and was so mortified by the e-mail that he didn't bother to call to follow up. It seemed a missed opportunity, but Sam tried hard not to think of it that way; otherwise he'd have to come to terms with how he'd screwed up the entire process right from the start.

When he got the text-message alert from The Open Note—another nice opt-in touch from Candace—letting him know that there would be a low-key networking opportunity the next night, he knew he had to go. Candace hadn't quite changed his life yet, but he found himself appreciating her approach. Like Roger, she was telling him that everything he was doing was wrong. Unlike Roger, she was showing him how to turn it around, one conversation at a time.

Sam swung by The Open Note early; it had become an enjoyable place to sort through e-mail and decompress from the day. Candace spotted him the moment he walked in, of course.

"Here for the roundtable?" she asked.

"Roundtable . . . ?" Sam said uncertainly.

"Conclave. Gathering. Get-together. Sometimes I refer to it as an Opening Circle. Not sure what exactly to call it, but it's become something of a ritual, a way for our members to be active resources and referral sources for one another and a way to build camaraderie and collegiality. Figured we could have a little fun, a few laughs, and start to make a few connections here."

"Who exactly is going to be here?" Sam ventured. "What companies are they with? I'd love to know a little more ahead of time to be able to—"

"That's quite enough of that," Candace said. "Don't treat this as an exercise in gathering business cards. Relax. Stretch out. Let the moment breathe."

"Let the moment breathe? No offense, Candace, but that sounds a little too crunchy granola for me."

"There's money in crunchy granola too, smart guy," she replied.

Sam smiled and took the hint. He spent the next hour in the routine, mundane tasks of twenty-first-century digital life: responding to e-mail, clicking a link or two, checking in on Facebook and LinkedIn.

As the sun set, Sam noticed how The Open Note changed its character as well. Candace made some subtle alterations to the atmosphere, such as changing the music. During the day it was unobtrusive, gentle adult-contemporary hits everyone knew and appreciated. In the late afternoon, she might bring in a classical guitarist, but as the night rolled in, the music became more peppery, more daring, more bass thumping, more psychedelic pop. Sam realized it when he noticed that he didn't know any of the last few songs that had been playing, but he was unconsciously tapping his foot anyway.

The overall effect wasn't to transform The Open Note into a boisterous party joint but to signal that the workday was done and it was time to change out of your dress clothes. You were likely to smile a little more openly, speak a little more freely than you would in a judgmental work environment.

"So?" Candace said as the streetlights out front flickered into life. "When are you going to join us?"

"Join . . . ?" Sam looked around. The Open Note had plenty of people scattered around on its leather couches and chairs, and almost none of them were in buttoned-down business attire. They weren't checking their phones or tapping away on laptops. The "event," Sam realized, had started without his being aware of it.

"This is the other side of The Open Note," Candace said, doing her best imitation of an infomercial host. "We're not just a coffee shop. We're not just a coworking space. We're a destination. A crossroads. A haven where professionals can come work or network or unwind. We've got conference rooms, workspaces, everything the rising professional needs outside the office. And we also have content and connections."

"I know. I remember the tour you gave me. It is lovely," Sam said. "Also quite a bit more expensive than a cup of coffee."

"That's true. There's also quite a bit more value that you get for participating here," Candace allowed, "but you will have to experience that firsthand to realize that for certain. How about being a guest member for the rest of this month on me? After that, if you discover that I'm right about the value, we can discuss a membership plan that works for you. How does that sound?"

"Like a warm chocolate chip cookie," Sam said, and Candace smiled as she led him to the larger group.

"Everyone, I'd like you to meet Sam," Candace said to the loosely gathered group around him. "Sam, this is Allen, Rebecca, . . ." Candace pointed to one person, then another, and listed their names as easily and warmly as if she were unfurling a family tree. Sam didn't remember a single one of them even though he tried, he really tried.

"A pleasure to meet all of you," Sam said automatically.

"Sam is a lawyer," Candace said, and a few good-natured boos came from the group, which numbered about ten. "Quiet," Candace continued. "You never know when you're going to need a good lawyer."

Sam saw what she was doing, and he appreciated it. She was giving him her implicit stamp of approval, vouching for him in a way that could pay dividends down the road. He didn't know any of these people, though, didn't know where they worked or how they'd ended up here. He was so deep into trying to divine the secret origins of his new compatriots that he almost completely missed what Candace was asking him to do.

". . . us a little about yourself," she said. "Sam?"

"Hmmm? Oh, right." Should he stand up? He was halfway to standing up when he paused, realized he looked ridiculous in that half crouch, kept on going, and finally stood stiffly in the middle of the room.

"This isn't a book report, Sam," Candace said. "Sit down. Relax."

"Good; I didn't read the book," he said with a little theatricality. "Felt like I was back in high school for a second there." He got a couple of chuckles from the group.

"Anyway, like Candace said, I'm an attorney," he continued. "I'm with Habersham & Smith just a couple blocks from here. My specialties are employment contracts and noncompete agreements, though I have done some commercial litigation and could certainly refer you to one of my senior partners should you, heaven forbid, need anything more serious. I'll leave a few of my business cards right here—" Sam was speaking in a rush, so he paused to pull a too-large stack of business cards from his pocket.

"What's your phone number, Sam?" Candace asked as he was fanning out the cards on the woodblock table in front of him.

"It's easy to remember," Sam said, and reeled off the catchy number. Then he looked up, saw Candace and everyone smiling at him, and realized what was going on.

"You didn't really want my phone number, did you?"

"No, Sam." Candace smiled. "Despite my mock infomercial earlier, this isn't a commercial, though thank you very much for providing us with one. I'll bill you later."

"Sorry," Sam said. "Didn't mean to turn it in that direction."

"Not a problem at all," Candace said, smoothing over the last of the awkwardness. "Tonight we're kicking around how to build relationships with the private equity community. Or at least that's the topic we'll start with. We may end up talking wine or movies or something completely unconnected along the way."

Sam nodded in understanding, though a part of him was screaming, So what is the point of this, then? I can talk wine or movies with anyone! But he stilled himself and willed himself to listen to Candace and the rest of these folks. Hey, it was only one night, right?

Sam talked a bit about himself—really talked—about his career and his background. He didn't veer into therapy territory—no sense confessing his sins to a bunch of people he didn't know and might need in a business capacity at some point down the line—but he did air out a few of his concerns about networking.

"I'm just not quite sure what to do, you know?" he said. "I mean, I want to get right to the heart of the matter way too fast."

"You were the kind of guy in high school who tried to get the good-night kiss before you'd even gotten out of her parents' driveway, am I right?" Candace laughed.

"I guess." Sam smiled. "I'm just afraid they're going to wriggle off the hook."

"Well, that's the problem right there," someone said. "Don't think of it as a hook. Think of it as a conversation."

"A conversation? With a fish?" someone else replied. "Yeah, that'll work."

"The whole fishing metaphor doesn't work," Candace said. "If you let that fish go after catching it, how do you know if you'll catch it again? And if you do decide to fry it up, you're definitely not catching it again. Your relationship with *that* particular fish is at its end."

"So how do you do it, Candace?" someone asked.

Candace waved a hand around the room. "You're all here, aren't you? How'd you get here? Did I beat you over the head by telling you to come? Did I try to shove a scone in your face?"

"No, but feel free to," someone piped up, and the group laughed.

"Not a chance." Candace smiled. "The trick to making connections is . . ." She paused, taking in the reactions of the group. Some leaned forward in anticipation; others sat back knowing what was coming.

"The trick to making connections is, there is no trick." She saw the disappointment flicker across some faces, including Sam's. "Seriously? You really thought there was some kind of magic formula for making better, stronger connections?"

"Well, we were kind of hoping . . ."

"Hope and three dollars will buy you a cup of coffee over there," Candace said. "Speaking of which, anybody need a refill?" A couple of hands went up.

Candace circled the group, serving up decaf and tea. It was growing late, after all. "The way to think about this is to reframe what you want out of a contact," she said. "If all you want is one transaction, then boom, that's easy. I could do that very easily here. A coupon here, a drive-through window there, and thanks for the money. But that's not what we're after here. We're after longer-term relationships, the kind that pay dividends without feeling like they're paying dividends."

The group nodded, but everyone remained quiet, and the hesitancy was palpable in the room.

Candace took matters into her own hands. "Sam, you're the new guy," she said, and this time he was paying attention. "Tell everybody how you go about making a contact."

"Usually," Sam said, "I wait till one gets dropped in my mouth like a baby bird getting fed by its mama." The group laughed, not unkindly.

"And how often does that happen, possible clients getting dropped in your open beak? Seems like that could be a bit demeaning."

"It's a little awkward," Sam laughed, "and it doesn't happen all that often. In fact, less and less each day."

"Exactly," Candace said. "And you know what I'm going to say next, don't you?"

"I've got a pretty good idea."

Candace motioned out the window at the now-quiet city streets. "All day long people walk up and down those streets, right outside my front door. They're close enough to touch—close enough for me to grab!—but if they don't have a reason to come in, they won't even bother. They've got much more important problems in their lives than worrying about whether some local indie coffee shop stays in business."

"So you lure them in with cookies," someone said, and Sam remembered how that maneuver had worked on him.

"Cookies, or tea, or music, or a book signing, or whatever brings value to the right people," Candace said. "You can't be all things to all people, but you can be everything to a few people. And that's what we're after here. Sometimes it takes just one contact to open doors everywhere for us."

"But how do we know it's the right contact?" Sam asked, and Candace nodded knowingly.

"Sam has had a bit of experience with the wrong contacts," Candace said. "Want to share, Sam? Give everyone a look at what not to do?"

"Thanks so much," Sam said sarcastically, but the tone of the room made it clear that everyone here almost surely had had a similar experience of his or her own. "Well, it began with me not knowing whether my contact was a man or a woman." The winces in the crowd were of sympathy.

Sam told the stories of Alex and Jordan then, making himself the well-deserved butt of the joke. And when he was done, when he'd laid out just what he'd done wrong, it seemed obvious to him. He almost wanted to get up from his chair and get back in circulation right then and there.

"So what was the issue, everybody?" Candace asked. "Wrong approach, obviously. But also . . . wrong contacts?"

"You need a referral source who can give you a little more than just a name," someone said. "You need someone who can tell you about the person, at least more than just their marital status and alumni affiliations. You need someone who can give you a heads-up on the personality and likely reaction of whoever it is you want to meet, about their situation."

"Absolutely," Candace said. "When we're done with this little get-together, anybody that wants to can connect on LinkedIn and Facebook. And if we don't have at least five friends of friends in this room, I'll—"

"Buy coffee at Starbucks?" someone said.

Candace sighed theatrically. "For you people, I'd do it. No, I'm serious. The average person has over 200 Facebook friends and over 300 LinkedIn connections. And rising professionals like you guys have way more. The numbers are in my favor here—you folks simply must have some mutual friends and opportunities for connections. So get those smartphones out, everyone, and start friending each other."

The meeting broke into a series of small conversations soon afterward, and as Sam was starting to pack up, Candace approached him with another gentleman. Twenty- or thirty-something and good-looking, he had a mannerly air about him and was wearing an immaculate golf shirt and slacks. "Sam, this is Allen Frazier," Candace said. "Allen is VP for technology at Thunderstick Technologies. Allen knows everybody, and he was just telling me he might be able to get you back in with Alex."

"Is that right?" Sam said. "Boy, that would be something."

"Alex and I went to business school together," Allen said. "She's probably been laughing about her call with you. Not in her nature to hold grudges. Maybe we can schedule lunch next week."

And just like that, Sam realized that Candace's ulterior motive might actually be working in his favor. He spent the next hour chatting up the fellow members of his group, and by the time he packed up to go, he'd found seven friends of friends through his various social network links. He'd booked lunches and drinks for two weeks. The idea of engaging with more of the right connections was still a fast-moving highway, but at least now he was moving parallel to the flow of traffic.

As he left, Sam made sure to catch Candace's eye. "Sign me up," he said, and she gave him a happy thumbs-up.

PLAN YOUR
DRAFT PICKS

10

Coach's Commentary

Connecting with the right people means more than just having them in your LinkedIn list and hoping they'll introduce you to prospects. It's better to *start* with your top prospects and then circle back to friends who can help you get connected. Who is at the top of Sam's prospect wish list besides whatever random company Roger throws his way? No one, that's who. Who is on yours? Candace understands the powerful link between having a well-considered prospect list in the form of a curated set of connections and achieving long-term success in business development.

⤳ OPENING

Right Connections + Right Conversations + Right Context

It's like the National Football League draft. The link between NFL draft success and long-term team success produces intense war room planning initiatives in which players are assessed and prioritized relative to the areas of strength and depth a team needs to build. The smart NFL teams make a wish list of the big playmakers and game-changing difference makers they will target, as well as other players who can make an impact and will fit and complement the existing team. They evaluate myriad variables, scenarios, and what-ifs, including the probability of actually landing a top pick and how to reprioritize if a competitor suddenly swipes their next choice.

Most significantly, the smartest teams don't dismiss undervalued and underappreciated players who may come up in later draft rounds but who can make a meaningful difference to the team. Jimmy Johnson, the former coach of the Dallas Cowboys, built his team into a dynasty in the 1990s by using a strategy in which players chosen in lower rounds were highly valued. With a stockpile of draft picks, he could create exactly the team he wanted while all the other teams were scrambling to figure out how to pay their number one picks.

Is this the way Sam manages his client, prospect, and referral pool? Not even close. Sam seems concerned only with the immediately evident people he knows or those who are sent his way and who he hopes can buy from him now. Although Sam's network may include people who can pay for his services right now, it is at least as full of rich sources of introductions, insights, and information advantage that raise his odds of winning more than his fair share of work. Here's a more productive, programmatic way that Sam, you, and I can use to make the most of our connections for business development purposes:

1. **Prioritize client and prospect organizations** and their most important executives.

2. **Cultivate your relationship inventory,** growing the willingness and ability of your connections to help you penetrate your wish list.

3. **Harvest introductions, insights, and information** that give you an unfair advantage.

Focus first on prioritizing your clients and prospects and the individuals you connect with in those organizations. In an NFL draft war room, a team may classify its player wish list by tiers—elites, blue chips, and red chips—on the basis of their ability, readiness, and predicted impact:

- **Elites** are draft pick candidates expected to immediately shine as top-ranking players in their positions and to be early Pro Bowl invitees.

- **Blue chips** are draft pick prospects whose talent and prior performance foretell early team-changing contributions.

- **Red chips** are picks viewed as players who have high potential but who may take slightly longer to evolve fully or who have unique skills such as special teams expertise.

Revised slightly, a similar set of categories can be applied to your business development client and prospect wish list. Although you may place opportunistic prospects—those who are referred to you without prompting or who simply stumble upon you—in one of these tiers, your tiered prospect wish list is really meant to include organizations that you have thoughtfully chosen and wish to pursue on purpose:

- **Gold tier.** These are your best existing clients, your "elites," your key clients of choice who offer the highest probability of additional relationship and revenue growth for you. You can call them by a different name if you want as long as you recognize them as your highest opening priority. Yes, the relationship is already "open," but that's like saying the door to the vault is cracked a hair's width open and there's a treasure inside. Keep opening the relationship and make sure it stays open.

- **Blue tier.** These are prospects whom you intentionally identify and who will make a major difference to your business when they become clients. Blue tier targets should match your client-of-choice profile and present the highest probability of opening into strong relationships and consequent revenue within a relatively short time frame. These are next on your opening priority list.

- **Red tier.** These are high-value prospects who provide reason to believe that they'll convert to client status though they may take slightly longer to evolve fully or who have strategic value to your organization or practice.

- **Orange tier.** Two types of organizations fit into the orange tier. These are clients who are profitable to maintain but offer limited growth potential. It also includes prospects with one-time or short-term engagement potential.

PRIORITIZE CLIENTS

Start with your existing clients. Which ones present the greatest potential to grow the relationship, add value, and increase revenue? It is a well-worn marketing truth that the fastest, most profitable way to generate new revenue is to keep and grow your current clients. Put your high-growth-potential existing clients at the top of your priority list: the gold tier.

Here's how you can tell if they are gold tier material:

They follow your advice and treat you like a partner rather than a vendor.

They're very profitable for you to serve and make a meaningful contribution to your overall revenue.

There's potential to grow the relationship and revenue further.

You can identify at least one of these four client growth strategies to guide your near-term efforts with that organization:

- You will especially focus on delivering more of the same services you've been delivering to the client within the same area (such as to the same team, department, geography, or business unit) you've been serving.

- You will especially focus on delivering the same services you've been delivering to a different area of the same client.

- You will especially focus on delivering new or different services from those you've delivered before to the same area of the client you previously have served.

- You will especially focus on delivering new or different services from what you've delivered before to an area of the client that you have never before served.

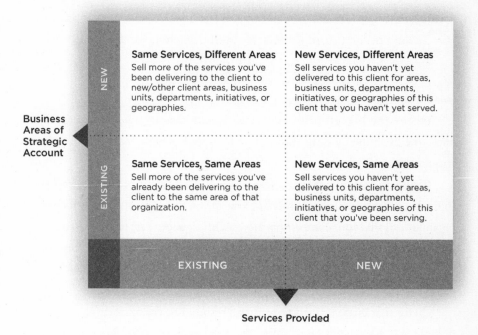

Business Areas of Strategic Account

NEW

Same Services, Different Areas
Sell more of the services you've been delivering to the client to new/other client areas, business units, departments, initiatives, or geographies.

New Services, Different Areas
Sell services you haven't yet delivered to this client for areas, business units, departments, initiatives, or geographies of this client that you haven't yet served.

EXISTING

Same Services, Same Areas
Sell more of the services you've already been delivering to the client to the same area of that organization.

New Services, Same Areas
Sell services you haven't yet delivered to this client for areas, business units, departments, initiatives, or geographies of this client that you've been serving.

EXISTING   NEW

Services Provided

IDENTIFY AND PRIORITIZE PROSPECT ORGANIZATIONS

Next, develop a prioritized wish list of prospects. If you struggle with this, you're not alone, but you're not excused either. Even if most of your work has been referred to you, that doesn't mean you shouldn't specifically identify and articulate a prospect wish list. At a minimum, providing your referral sources with specific target organization and executive names better equips them to refer you to those or similar companies.

Earlier, you created a detailed description of your ideal client. You listed the statistics, similarities, and situations that define your targets. Use those criteria as a checklist to search for and uncover the organizations in your market that match them.

Identify the top companies in your market that are most likely to be attracted by your positioning (not just the ones you most want as a client but, more important, those who would most want *you* to support them).

Specify the highest-probability prospects by name and also specify by name the executives within those companies with whom you need to build strong relationships.

Where do you find companies that should be on your prospect wish list, those that fit your ideal client criteria? How do you find hidden prospects: those organizations that your competitors may not know about yet? How do you find hidden opportunities: situations that trigger the need for your service that you identify before your competitors do? The answers lie in where you look—your sources—and how you look—your questions—for the information.

Quarterbacks are trained to read and respond to complex defensive formations and movements under stress. You need to do the same thing, although the consequences of a misread on your part are unlikely to include bodily injury at the hands of a Neanderthal linebacker.

Your job is to read the market and your prospect's circumstances and see the unspoken implications that lie beneath the tangible facade of facts.

Don't accept what's publicly presented as the whole situation. What is missing? What might that absence of information mean? Be a change detective—unearth the imminent changes facing your prospects before anyone else does. Follow the money—consider the economic impacts of the shifts they're encountering. Be a forensic detective—ponder the details, researching the nuances and communicating the risk and value of changes.

Change is your friend. When a major change occurs in one of your target clients, it could open an opportunity for the organization to change the professional and business services firms with which it most associates. But you need an early detection system to let you know when that type of change takes place. A programmatic process consists of you or someone on your team regularly searching select information sources with detailed questions that increasingly uncover usable insights. For some samples of the criteria, sources, and questions that may guide your efforts, see the three accompanying figures.

CLIENT OF CHOICE STATISTICS

SEARCH CRITERIA	SOURCES	QUESTIONS
Statistics	**Tools to Find Organizations That Fit**	**What to Ask Yourself**
Includes criteria like:	*Examples:*	*Examples:*
• Industry • Annual revenue • Number of employees • Headquarters location • Decision maker title	• Industry association membership directories • Company lists from business and industry specific publications • Company news from business and industry specific publications • Industry insider blogs • Google search • LinkedIn search • Twitter search • Specialized industry directories • Chambers of commerce directories • Foreign trade consulates and chambers	• Where can I find the most current and comprehensive list of organizations with these key attributes? • Who else serves this industry—other advisors and suppliers—with whom I can compare prospect lists?

CLIENT OF CHOICE SIMILARITIES

SEARCH CRITERIA	SOURCES	QUESTIONS
Similarities	**Tools to Find Organizations That Fit**	**What to Ask Yourself**
Includes criteria like:	*Examples:*	*Examples:*
• Organizational similarities • Corporate alumni • Military service • School alumni • Business, sports, country club • Not-for-profit boards • Industry associations • Rare achievements (e.g., Eagle Scouts) • Hometown • Political affiliation • Religious affiliation • Other personal attributes	• Corporate and academic websites and directories • Corporate and academic alumni groups on LinkedIn and other social media sites • Not-for-profit website board of directors lists • Industry association and local chapter website boards of directors lists • LinkedIn "interest" search • Organization website executive bios	• Which organizations are led by executives with whom I share a strong area of affinity? • Which ones are led by people who previously worked at the same company I did? • Which ones have leaders who went to the same schools I attended? • Which ones have leaders who share the same interests, activities, associations, etc. as me?

CLIENT OF CHOICE SITUATIONS

SEARCH CRITERIA	SOURCES	QUESTIONS
Situations	**Tools to Find Organizations That Fit**	**What to Ask Yourself**
Includes criteria like:	*Examples:*	*Examples:*
• Mergers and acquisitions	• Public data—about shifts, lawsuits, etc.	• Who would see this situation ahead of you?
• New investors	• Economic development officials	• What are the implications of the latest news about this organization?
• Newly hired executives		
• Headquarters relocation	• Curiosity like a journalist or an academic	• What else might this news mean?
• Regulatory changes	• Listening for shifts	• What needs does this situation create?
• Major lawsuit	• Ask other service providers	
• Initial public offering		• Which executives are ripe for promotion or for poaching, and which are static or slipping?
• Bankruptcy		
• Hypergrowth		

There are plenty of online tools that provide ongoing information about market movements such as the ones listed here. You can, for example, keep tabs on a prospect by following it through Google Alerts. Twitter may provide early company announcements and investor reports. The best early warning system, though, isn't digital. It's human.

Prioritizing Prospect Executives

The first thing you need to know about prioritizing which prospect executives you need to know and how you spend your time is this: if you know only one person at your target organization, you've got nothing to prioritize. Also, you're probably screwed. To effectively win work with anything but a one-person company, you need to build relationships with more than one person. Too many potential client engagements are lost because a professional sat smugly believing he or she had it locked up. That professional had one friend in the prospect company who was allegedly the decision maker and thought that was enough. Only after he or she lost the opportunity to a competitor did the professional learn that several others were involved or influenced the decision. One prospect executive, perhaps one you didn't even know existed, happened to have a family member or best friend who was one of your main competitors. It's going to go down like that very often unless you surround the prospect organization.

You need to know the decision makers, yes. You also need to know who influences the decision. That's true too. And you need to know other informed insiders who can give you insight and advice about the prospect's situation, about pricing expectations, about the political dynamics involved, and about the personalities of the players. That could be someone in the prospect organization who is not at all involved with the decision but who is wired into the company information flow. It could be another third-party provider who serves the prospect organization and is willing to provide perspective.

Further, you will uncover and build a variety of relationships with each of these prospect executive types. You may have a former client or past coworker in the prospect company. They've experienced you firsthand, and assuming their impression of you was positive, they're at the top of your priority list. There may be prospect executives with whom you have a good common connection and to whom you were personally recommended. They're next in line. There may simply be someone on the prospect side with whom you share a strong affinity—a common background or interest or experience—and that may be enough to help you establish a useful relationship with that person.

Between the prospect executive's role in the decision to hire folks like you and the nature of your relationship with that person, your priorities are revealed. The accompanying figure shows how this shakes out. As in Bingo, if you have only one chip on the board, your odds of winning aren't so good. Your objective is to fill the board.

PROSPECT PEOPLE PRIORITIZATION

	DECISION	INFLUENCE	INSIGHT
CLIENT	PRIORITY 1	4	7
CONNECTION	2	5	8
AFFINITY	3	6	9

RESPECT YOUR FRONT LINE

11

Roll Game Film

The Cherry Blossom Golf & Country Club had one of the finest courses in the area, a rolling, verdant expanse that had hosted dozens of Professional Golfers' Association (PGA) tournaments. An invitation to play Cherry Blossom was an indication that you'd arrived, and you'd better recognize and celebrate that fact.

Sam couldn't celebrate anything. He was too busy trying to keep down his lunch. He'd come out to the course with Roger and two longtime clients, knowing full well what awaited him, and on the seventeenth green the hammer dropped.

"So I've got to tell you a story about our boy Sam here," Roger began, and from there it just got ugly. Roger recounted Sam's disastrous meeting with Joe Jordan and his humiliating attempt at landing Alex Itzikoff's business, and the clients cackled away. They slapped him on the back with you'll-get-'em-next-time-kid chortles, but Sam noticed that none of the three shared any embarrassing client stories of their own. Sam was twisting in the wind alone.

As they drove to the eighteenth tee, Roger leaned over to Sam and smiled. "You realize this means I'm not going to waste any more of my big-time leads on you," he said, laughing in that painful we-both-know-I'm-not-kidding way. He clapped Sam hard on the knee, then pointed out toward the water surrounding the eighteenth green.

"There are alligators out there, Sam," he said.

"Sir, I don't think there are alligators in this part of the country—"

"Not *there*, Sam. All around our business. Alligators. And they have to be fed. They have names, Sam. Do you know what their names are?"

This was sounding like a children's lesson, and frankly, Sam wasn't pleased with it. He tried to keep his voice calm because he knew Roger was looking for an answer. "What are their names, Roger?"

"Their names are Rent. And Utilities. And Staff Holiday Parties. And all the other overhead that we have to come up with to keep the office running before we get our draws. You have to feed those alligators before you can take anything for yourself, Sam. Because believe me, when the alligators come to your door, they're going to eat whatever's around. And that includes you."

Sam tried hard not to let his eyes roll all the way around in his head.

After the round was over, the foursome unwound in the course's grill room. Sam was keeping Candace's ideas in his head—don't jab these guys for business, keep the conversation moving—when a silver-haired gentleman in a golf shirt that must have once fit him well approached their table. He and Roger knew each other and traded pleasantries. Then Roger turned to Sam.

"Chuck, this is Sam Wentworth. He's a good kid."

"This your boy?" Chuck said, starting a hearty handshake.

"No, no, he's one of our associates," Roger said, and Sam could feel the handshake diminish. "Knows a thing or two. He could help you guys out."

"That so," Chuck said, clearly ready to be done with this line of conversation. "Good to meet you, Sam."

"And you, sir," Sam said, careful not to venture anything that might expose his utter ignorance of this man and his business.

"You see that?" Roger said as Chuck—no last name as far as Sam could tell—walked away from the table. "I'm getting you leads left and right! Run with 'em, son!"

Sam ran, all right—he ran all the way to The Open Note, where he slumped into a chair in the large coworking common area (he had signed on as a full-fledged member) and sighed heavily at the thought of the debacle that was that day.

"But was the golf good at least?" Allen asked with a smile.

"No! I was so nervous about screwing something up that I put two sleeves of balls into the woods. I've got to tell you, Allen, I'm just fed up with having to make nice all the time and kiss up to these older guys for business. How do you do it? How do you keep glad-handing day after day?"

"Well, don't think about it as glad-handing, for starters," Allen said. "People can sense when you're open to new meetings, new connections. People want to know what you have to offer, and if you don't have something to offer them—"

"You get Chuck's dead-fish routine."

"Bingo. And you know why that guy didn't care about you? Because he *didn't have a reason to care*. He was all over you when he thought you were your partner's kid. He and your partner, they can do business. But you? You're another young face in the crowd. There've been a thousand before you, and there'll be a thousand after you."

"You know how to make a guy feel unique," Sam said.

"I'm not here to make you feel good about yourself." Allen grinned. "That's Candace's job. I'm here to give you the truth as I see it. You don't look like you have much to offer when you're all slumped down and defeated."

Candace swooped over to check in on the two. "There's more to it than posture," she said. "You've got to make sure to communicate what makes you famous. And you've got to make sure others know it, too."

"Famous." Sam laughed. "Worst business developer in the history of my firm. How's that? What's the opposite of a rainmaker?"

"You're fishing, Sam," Candace said. "You know what you have to offer. And clearly, your partner doesn't. If people are going to make introductions on your behalf," she continued, turning to look at Allen, "they've got to know what they're introducing."

"I'm happy to help," Allen said. "Let's see what we can do about digging into your network."

Sam pulled out his laptop and opened a file titled "COMPANIES." On it were listed a dozen firms, some large, some small. No people attached, just company names.

"What's this?" Candace asked.

"It's my list of target companies," Sam replied.

"No, it's not," Candace said. "It's a holiday wish list. There's no connection here, no cohesion. Why these companies?"

Allen scrolled through the list. "I know people here, and here, and here," he said. "I can get in the door." He reached for his phone, but Candace told him to wait.

"Before we get to that point," she said, "just give us the names. Sam, write these down."

Allen rattled off the names of executives he knew at each of the companies, and Sam dutifully typed each one next to the company's name.

"Perfect," Candace said, and the two men nodded in approval. Then Candace pointed at the screen.

"Now, erase that."

"What? But we just—"

"Erase it."

Sam did, breathing a heavy sigh. "What now?"

"Now," Candace said, "you start telling Allen and me what we need to know to best represent you to those contacts. Worry about who you are and what you have to offer before you start thinking about who you're going to contact."

"But what about—"

Candace held up a hand. "Don't even start. Making a list of companies is nice. Making a list of people is also nice. But if you don't know exactly what your claim to fame is, it's like setting out without a map. Worse, if you try to get people to intercede on your behalf, it's like meeting a date over the telephone. There's plenty you're missing out on by not describing yourself, your practice, your claim to fame more fully."

So Sam talked. He talked about his background, his skills as a litigator and as a mediator, his interest in everything from soccer to James Bond movies. He made sure that Allen understood the many ways Sam could help a company, the many ways Sam had something to offer.

"That's the key," Candace said. "Think about Alex who's really Alexis. Why should she spend any more time even thinking about you? Why should she bother with you since you screwed up the first attempt so badly? What does she have to gain from giving you—or you via your proxy, Allen—a few minutes of her time even if she decides not to hire you?"

"Uh . . . I'm a good lawyer?"

Candace scowled at him. "Seriously? That's all you can come up with? Think, Sam. Think more about yourself and what you have to offer that can make you more of an attractive commodity, more like someone people *want* to spend time getting to know. 'I'm a good lawyer' isn't it."

For the next half hour Sam did just that, thinking hard about the ways in which he could distinguish himself from his competition, his fellow "good lawyers." When he'd finished, when he'd completed a total self-evaluation that somehow left him feeling both better and worse about himself, he stood up to go.

"I've got to get out of here." Sam sighed. "I'm ragged." He shook Allen's hand and reached to shake Candace's. She turned to Allen again with a sharp nod of her head.

"First lesson in dealing with people who can bring you business," Candace said. "Don't treat them any worse than you treat your clients. Remember, they're not disposable. They're a vital part of your overall inventory of relationships. And they can bring you some amazingly good returns . . . if you keep treating them well."

Sam nodded and smiled. "Allen, you have been a treasure," he said, and Allen laughed. "I'll invite you and your family up to my summer home as soon as I have one."

"Deal." Allen laughed. "I'll start the ball rolling with Alex tomorrow."

"See how easy it is?" Candace said. "Now, both of you don't leave without paying."

BE A BETTER
TEAMMATE

12

Coach's Commentary

Any business endeavor that succeeds has to overcome dozens, even hundreds of hurdles. Logistical, financial, bureaucratic . . . no matter how imposing these hurdles seem, they all boil down to a single element: relationships. As we've discussed before, build relationships and you build the foundation for a successful business. Rivers flow only one way. Relationships shouldn't. Make sure that your best referral sources know exactly how much you value them.

Consider this: in 2013, Minnesota Vikings running back Adrian Peterson bought his offensive linemen snowmobiles to thank them for their assistance in helping him craft one of the best individual seasons in NFL history in 2012. That's a pretty tangible way of demonstrating just how valuable someone is to your own efforts and how much you value that person's contribution to your life and your business. Now, you don't necessarily have to come up with snowmobiles, particularly if you live anywhere south of Minnesota, but you ought to consider the best ways you can reward those who have helped you along the way. There are no assumptions, no givens in referrals; do right by them, and they'll continue to do right by you.

Note the ways in which Candace taps her own inventory of relationships to grow The Open Note through word of mouth (and text, and Facebook, and Twitter, and so forth). How does one carve out a space in a crowded marketplace? By distinguishing oneself and by making sure everyone nearby knows exactly what that distinction is.

Remember, Candace views The Open Note not just as a way for her clientele to get great coffee and pastries, though that's certainly its initial drawing card. No, walk deeper into the café and you'll see Candace's true vision: a way to serve entrepreneurs' and rising professionals' need for networking and knowledge. The Open Note is designed as an informal environment for this express reason: to help create and strengthen connections between people who all too often can feel disconnected in our current wireless society.

The Open Note's customers are its best forms of advertising. A professional who finds both spiritual regeneration and financial remuneration from a visit to The Open Note has every reason to spread the word about its many benefits. And it's not just people who walk in the front door; Candace can connect with those who come in the back door—the suppliers—to create additional value for herself and her enterprise.

Let's drill down to the heart of this. What are the differences between prospects and referrals? Prospects are the targets of a direct relationship, a direct campaign. You seek out and cultivate prospects yourself. Referrals, in contrast, involve a middle party of some sort. They're indirect relationships. You don't have direct control over the process, which means you have to be even more prepared—and, it must be noted, arm your referral sources with even more information about yourself.

Referral relationships can be loose, in which case you connect only when you or your contact has a potential client on the line and needs help reeling it in. Or referral relationships can be more formalized: a monthly meeting to discuss leads, options, and strategies, perhaps.

Neither approach is universally better than the other; both are dependent on your referral contact's willingness and ability to help. A willing referrer with no contacts may be a pleasant conversation partner but not much in the way of a business possibility. Likewise, a well-connected referrer with little interest in spreading the wealth can be a tough nut to crack.

An opening isn't designed for you to connect with every person in your desired industry. It's not a wide net. It's the tip of the spear, the way to focus your effort on the most useful referrers, the people who can help you (and, you hope, whom you in turn can help) get in the door, and on the most consequential clients of choice: those whose doors you want to enter.

Thus, you need to do a little prequalification with your referrers. Relax. This isn't like trying to prequalify for a home loan; there's no need to provide reams of documents. But the basic principle is the same: demonstrate that you're a valuable contact, someone worth knowing. More important, equip your contact with the information he or she needs to represent you fairly and accurately. The worst thing possible would be to have a perfect referral foiled because a referrer failed to give an accurate accounting of your qualifications or specialties.

Thus, you need to be able to distinguish among referral source relationships and act accordingly. We break down referral sources into two major groups: preferred and promiscuous. You can see where this is going:

Preferred sources can deliver you more value on a consistent basis. Promiscuous sources may deliver once in a while, but you can't count on them for continuous value.

You don't want to close the door on promiscuous referral sources, but you definitely don't want to spend too much time focusing on them at the expense of your preferred ones.

Thus, consider how to build your own network of preferred referral sources. Who has already scoured the market for prospects like the ones you're seeking? Whose names come up most often in networking conversations? Whose names are mentioned most frequently when you need information or insight on a particular industry topic? Listen with the right ears and you'll be able to discern the people with whom you should connect.

From there, it's a matter of building the foundation. Your options are only as limited as your imagination. You could create an industry community, a referral group of expert resources who may serve clients such as yours but don't directly compete with you. You could compare prospect lists, seeing where there's affinity and where there's the possibility for a friend-of-a-friend connection.

Let's go back to the coach metaphor. Just as a good coach knows the strengths of each of his or her players, not just positionally but situationally, you should be aware of your contacts' referral potential. Who works best in face-to-face meetings; who works best in informal networking environments? Who's got a decent golf game, a knowledge of wine, an appreciation for art that can be brought to bear in the course of business development? These aren't small questions. The more you are willing to learn about your referral sources in order to help them, the more likely they are to reciprocate. You owe one another that level of diligence if you are to be more help than harm.

Your ideal referral sources are equally knowledgeable about your strengths, your needs, and your potential clients' ability to connect with those strengths and needs. They need to know the right information about you, and they need to know how that information matches up with your referral sources' needs. In a sense, they're playing matchmaker for you, and you want to look your best in any such situation. It takes only one poorly timed or poorly worded referral to sink your chances with a potential client. Why would you take that chance?

Remember, though, that this isn't an adversarial situation.

In soccer, every player works with purpose to create better passing options and openings for the player on the ball. Consider your key connections to be your teammates.

Every one of them is a potential source of information, a way to be introduced to your ideal prospects. It's up to you to help them create those passing options by delivering both insights and relationship advantage with prime prospects. When they pass you the ball, you want to be ready to receive it, ready to drive, ready to score.

It's important to reiterate that we're doing everything we can to avoid the binary approach to introduction—the automatic yes or no. (Well, the automatic yes is just fine, but those are as rare as the sun rising in the west.) You're trying to open the door; you're not trying to get a referendum on yourself and your abilities right off the bat.

Let's make sure you are thinking as broadly as possible about who might make a good potential referral source, and then we can home in on the best resources. Here are some of your possibilities:

Existing clients. Current clients and those with whom you worked in the past may be able to refer you to prospects within or outside their own companies, but be sure to toe that professionalism line. Don't ruin what you already have.

Other professionals. Your colleagues in noncompetitive areas or organizations (such as other professional firms that serve the same types of clients you seek) could well have the ability to set you up with contacts that need your particular skill set.

Alumni. Former classmates as well as colleagues with whom you once worked can be excellent sources of information and contacts. They know your stories and skills and what you can deliver.

Community contacts. Family and friends, charitable and religious organizations, and educational/institutional relationships can be tricky as you may fear overstepping personal boundaries by engaging in business matters in these settings, but with the right perspective and the right touch, you can expand friendships to include a commercial component.

Remember, not every referral source is created equal. As wonderful as it is to have these sources, it's worth asking a few hard questions not of them but about them:

- How willing are they to help?

- How strong is their reputation? Yours will be enhanced or brought down in part by theirs.

- How strong are your affinities with that individual, both personal and professional?

- Have they actually made successful referrals on your (or anyone's) behalf in the recent past?

- How willing are you to help them in return?

The further along you proceed in your referral source development, the more you'll be able to quickly identify the quantitative and qualitative differences between potential referral sources. You'll be able to hone your set of sources to a more refined level. You'll also be able to develop more consequential relationships with higher-level sources, ones that can do you more good over longer periods.

Remember this: the most valuable referral sources should be treated as if they were clients. Take good care of them, and they'll take good care of you.

FIND OPEN RECEIVERS FAST

13

Roll Game Film

Sam and Allen met at The Open Note two days later, and Sam got to know Allen a bit better. Resisting the urge to badger him for contacts, Sam sat back and listened. Although Allen's story wasn't unique—worked his way up from humble origins, first in his family to go to college, relentless climber—what Sam realized was that Allen had exactly the kind of contact list Sam craved. Allen knew everyone. He played golf with the people Sam wanted to know. He attended the same parties as the people Sam needed to know. He'd amassed his roster of contacts with the kind of smooth grace that made it seem effortless.

"People are a lot more willing to give you their contact info if they think you're going to be giving something back," Allen said. "I try not to pester these people too much, if at all. You want them to trust you, to know that you're not going to be calling them up every week or pitching them on your latest site launch or whatever. They get enough of that."

"How do you segue from getting a contact into getting a deal, though? That's what I can't figure out."

"When you learn it," Allen said with a laugh, "let me know, okay?"

The comment struck Sam as a bit strange—surely someone with that kind of contact list had clients banging on his door—but he let it pass for the moment because Candace was approaching their table.

"My two favorite businessmen!" she gushed.

"You say that to everyone, don't you?" Allen smiled.

"Of course," Candace said. "But you love it, and you know it."

"No more cookies?" Sam said.

"By this point, you gentlemen ought to be getting your own cookies," Candace replied. "Are you two busy? Or do you have a moment?"

"For you, dear, anything," Allen said in a gooey-sweet voice, and Candace nodded. "Touché. I've got someone I want you both to meet."

She ushered over a finely dressed but slightly hesitant woman. Sam and Allen recognized her from their evening gatherings, but they'd never gotten to know her. She came and went in a hurry, without much conversation.

"Sam. Allen. I'd like you to meet Becca Kimani," Candace said. "Becca is an accountant—auditor, I believe—with McMillan MacArthur." At that, both Sam and Allen took a much greater interest. Mc-Mac, as it was affectionately called, was one of the city's legendary white shoe firms. Outside the Big Four accounting giants, McMillan MacArthur had a lock on the middle market and private equity–backed companies in town. Through her relationship with the firm, Becca was likely to be well connected.

Candace noticed their expressions change. "We've all got something everyone else wants at this table," she said. "Heck, everyone in The Open Note has something that we all could want, but it's not good form to just go up and ask them, is it? Here, though—here, things are safer and easier, because you've started to spend the time getting to know each other and understand what each other wants and needs."

"Tell us a little about yourself, Becca," Sam said, taking the handoff from Candace.

"Nothing too different from most of us all," Becca said. "My parents were Japanese-Filipino and became first-generation immigrants. They made sure I took advantage of every opportunity whether I wanted to or not. Princeton undergrad, master's in accounting from Wharton Business, out into the world and hitting the ground running."

"That's impressive," Allen said, and Sam nodded. "You're so young for getting so far. What brings you in here?"

Becca looked at Candace and smiled. "She's been my therapist, as I assume she has been for you too," Becca said.

"A lot cheaper, though," Sam said, and Allen mock shushed him.

"Next cookie's going to cost $75," Candace said.

Becca continued. "I've followed the correct path exactly," she said. "I've had no problem at all going from point A to point B."

"Excuse me just a second," Candace said. "Becca, would you mind showing them your briefcase?"

Becca smiled in slight embarrassment and turned her briefcase around to face the others. She held it open, and inside they could see an array of papers, supplies, and other office elements as neatly organized as a store's shelves. For Sam in particular, who treated his briefcase with all the grace of flinging laundry into a hamper, it was a revelation.

"How much time do you spend on that?" Sam said, his voice just short of wonder.

"Not as much as you'd think," Becca replied. "It's about ongoing maintenance. Keep it up every day and you soon find it's not that hard to do each individual day."

"You need to show me your secrets," Allen said. "I could use a little of that organization in my life too. But you left us hanging at point B."

"I went from point B to point C all the way to point Z," Becca said, "and frankly, I'm not quite sure what to do from here. I know exactly how to do what I'm supposed to do, but what happens when I don't know what I'm supposed to do?"

"Sounds familiar, doesn't it, Sam?" Candace said. "Becca is absolutely dedicated to the regimentation of the modern business world, but like so many other people, she's not quite sure what to do when there isn't regimentation."

"That's it exactly." Becca nodded. "I'd be happy to take on a new challenge, but I just don't know where that challenge might be, and I don't know where to find it. And frankly, I never feel like I can afford to spend the time on business development when I've got to put clients first."

"This is exactly where a mentor would come in," Allen said. "Is there anyone you can work with at your office? A senior partner, someone who could show you the ropes?"

"Careful with that," Sam said. "It doesn't always work the way you'd think it would."

"Fair enough," Allen said. "Still, I have to think we could find some kind of way for Becca to take that next step forward. I'd love to help you, but I have absolutely no idea what I'm doing when it comes to accounting. Balancing my checkbook is enough work for me."

"That's where I come in, then," Candace said. "I know each of you has contacts that you could use that could help the others get ahead. This is a big city, but it's not *that* big. And by now you three have more than a quarter century's combined work experience among you. So it's time to take another step forward. Get those laptops and smartphones out, everybody."

They did, in a tangle of cables and hardware.

"Here's the deal," Candace said. "The Open Note food truck is about to go on a run for a festival down by the river. It's stopping by here in 60 minutes. Until then, I want to see who among you can make the most of their most consequential connections for the others."

"Easy," Sam said. "Allen has us all smoked. We saw that when we put everything together the last time we were here."

"Allen knows plenty of people," Candace agreed. "But—no offense, Allen—just knowing people is only part of the battle. *Consequential* is the key word here. That means I want to see who has the most connections that are appropriate contacts for the other two of you. That means you need to know each other's claim to fame or Opening Strategy and what a great referral looks and sounds like for each other. What you need to be able to do is turn those names into relationships and put those relationships into motion for each other."

She passed out small menus for The Open Note's food truck. "So here's the deal. The winner is the one who's able to provide the most useful contacts to the other two. This is a contest where giving is getting. The winner gets lunch on the house, their choice. And if I do say so myself, this is a fine prize."

Candace left them to their work as she began prepping for the food truck. The three of them broke out their laptops and notepads and began to write. They set up their major social networks—LinkedIn and Facebook, of course, but also Google+, Twitter, and assorted smaller networks, as well as their standard contact list—and began to ripple their circles outward to see what connected with the others.

In short order, they were stuck. "I know people who are CFOs at companies, Becca," Sam said. "But I'm really not sure which ones would be most open to meeting with you or why they would." In the same way, Allen was confused. "Sam, same here for me. What kind of law do you practice again?" They then set about learning one another's Opening Stories and what types of circumstances and prospects moved their needle in a consequential way. They listed their desired client companies and worked through one another's lists to see who they might know at each of those companies. Then they broadened the search outward, working within their industry and then their geographic location and then the business situations in which they were most helpful to clients.

As they went on, each of them learned a lot about his or her contact list. Sam, for instance, learned that he had a lot of work to do to get his contacts in order and up to date. He was two jobs behind on some of them; others lacked basic information such as place of business or, in some cases of gender-neutral names, whether they were male or female. He looked with admiration at Allen's list, which was relentlessly well organized and managed. He had cross-referenced his contacts with multiple outlets, meaning he had a complete picture of everyone he needed to know. It was an impressive achievement, and Sam resolved to shape up his contact list in a hurry.

Becca's contact list was equally pristine, but it was almost criminally short. She had only a couple of dozen Facebook and LinkedIn connections, far fewer than she should have had at that stage in her career. With that in mind, Sam and Allen set to the task of beefing up her list with people they figured she'd need to know. They connected her, and each other, with the appropriate individuals in their respective lists. Then they examined one another's lists, trying to find where they had areas of convergence. Sure enough, they spotted some overlaps quickly.

When The Open Note food truck pulled up in front of the café—like the café, the truck was immaculate and quirky all at once—there was a clear winner in the lunch battle. Allen had definitively strengthened both Sam and

Becca's contact lists, and he'd provided them with half a dozen usable leads for improving both their client prospects and their careers. In a single hour's networking, he'd done more for them than either of them had done for himself or herself in several years.

So it was with gratitude that both Sam and Becca happily served Allen his lunch. He'd earned it, after all.

"What's next for you three?" Candace asked as the food truck rolled off to its destination.

"I'll be making a few calls on behalf of my friends," Allen said.

"And I'll be following up on those calls," Sam added.

"I'm going to plan out some time to make those calls too, and then I should be able to get to them in the next couple of days," put in Becca.

Candace looked at all three of them, seeing possibilities. "Sounds good. Allen, don't get so wrapped up making calls for others that you forget to handle your own. Sam, don't be so eager to call that you forget what we learned about understanding your connections. And Becca? Don't spend too much time planning for perfection. Ten percent thinking, ninety percent doing, okay?"

They all nodded in recognition of their own needs and resolved to do a better job picking up the slack where needed. It was a win all the way around.

MASTER THE LOCKER ROOM SPEECH

14

Coach's Commentary

Some of the most powerful speeches in life and on film are given in locker rooms. Whether it's the classic "Win one for the Gipper," which may or may not have actually been spoken by Knute Rockne, or the more recent speech by Al Pacino in *Any Given Sunday* ("Life is a game of inches . . . the inches we need are all around us"), the locker room speech inspires, strengthens, and endures. You may not have the gift of oratory of a Pacino or a Ronald Reagan (who played Rockne), but you can definitely up your conversational game and make yourself a figure around whom people will congregate. The locker room speech is a coach's scythe. With it, he reaps the harvest of hard work by inspiring extraordinary effort on the field. In business development, the harvest that you seek is in the form of credible connections. Just as a coach's locker room words and leadership presence can accelerate or derail a team's performance, the words you share with your referral sources and your actions and presence as a leader are the keys to the perfect introductions or the worst ones.

Coaches often tell their teams to remember the fundamentals. In the locker room before Super Bowl II in 1968, the legendary coach Vince Lombardi exhorted his Green Bay Packers to "just hit, just run, just block, and just tackle." The Packers won 33–14 over the Oakland Raiders. Fundamentals matter in eliciting the best referrals, too. Here are the six basics—words and actions—you need to elicit the best referrals.

LEARN

Be genuinely curious about your contacts if you want them to be curious about how they can help you. If you really care to learn about your referral sources, you'll make sure to care *in person* as often as possible. First off, get face to face. Can you imagine a locker room speech in which the content is delivered by e-mail or text message? Get out of the office and into the marketplace. Don't wait for referral sources to come to you. Instead, you need to stay visible, stay in sight, and let them know how open and enthusiastic you are about working with them. Get in circulation, make it happen, and keep it going forward. *Get open*. It's the motto of The Open Note food truck, it's a mantra for every wide receiver who has ever played the game of football, and it's a useful motto for anyone seeking to improve a client referral base.

You can't go into those in-person meetings cold, though. Learn about your referral sources before meeting with them. Be prepared by knowing who they know—who is in their network—and be able to articulate names and descriptions of preferred clients who are connected to them. You can find this out through LinkedIn, Google, or personal inquiries.

One other point: you can listen better. Everyone can. Pay attention to individuals and companies that your existing relationship mentions during the normal course of your conversations. Acting on specific contacts that your existing relationship already has will yield significantly better results than simply asking if someone can "introduce you to some good people."

MODEL

Show your referral sources how to do it right by giving a great referral or intro-duction *to* them before you expect to get one *from* them. Do this by learning about their claim to fame, their clients of choice, their points of affinity, and specifics about what value they may bring in an introduction you provide. Then show them how you use that information to make a compelling introduction on their behalf that ensures an open door. Modeling is not for quid pro quo purposes as much as it is for teaching your referral sources how a successful introduction is made. You show others where the bar is, and they'll try to clear it.

EQUIP

Help your referral sources be heroes by equipping them with the tools they need to make a successful connection for you. Share your Opening Story with them and remind them of it, but more important, bring it to life. Demonstrate it. That may mean providing them or their firm with an experience of what it is like to work with you: do for them what you do for your clients, perhaps on a small scale for a reduced rate or even gratis as a sample-size offering. Let them know your affinity and trigger points: the ways you best find common ground with others and the issues that cause a client to need your services. Give them the words to make a great introduction. Ask, "Would it be helpful if I can give you some points on what I've seen work best for me with referrals? What works for you?" Write the script (or introduction e-mail) for them if needed. Provide them with an enduring "just say yes" rationale for why their contact should meet with you. This will be a reason that goes beyond any near-term engagement of you by your referral source's contact. This will be a rationale for why that contact will benefit from spending his or her precious time with you even if he or she ends up buying nothing from you.

ASK

Ask for specific help with humility and respect. You must treat others' relationships with the respect you want for your own. Provide context, such as "My firm weathered the recession very well, and we're now trying to grow our practice to the next level." Then get to the point: "I could really use your help and have a favor to ask. Probably the best way to start a dialogue with prospective clients is to get connected through a mutually respected friend."

Sam has gotten used to asking for help like this: "If you know anyone who needs a lawyer, please keep me in mind." Well, that's one way to do it. You can imagine how this would go in the real world:

"So if I have a friend that needs a divorce, then you can help?"

"No."

"Oh, so I know a guy who has a barbershop that he wants to sell, so you could help him do that deal, right?"

"Well, yes, but . . ."

Instead, find out ahead of time which of your prospects of choice are linked to your referral source and ask directly about those individuals or organizations. Be specific: "X, Y, and Z are the types of companies/people where we are usually very helpful."

Then confirm the nature of your referral source's connection. "Are those companies/people you know well?" (*Note:* If you've done your homework, you know they are.)

Next, reveal your purpose. By that we mean that you've got to make sure your source knows why you're asking for an introduction. "I could use the business" isn't enough. "I was reading about some of the big changes in [target company/industry] and thinking about some of the work our firm has done to support other clients in similar situations. It appears [target company or executive name] may be dealing with some of those same changes. Perhaps I can be a sounding board for them."

You need to be specific about what you bring of value that would make it worthwhile for the other person to meet you. What exactly can you provide that would be worthwhile for your source to pass along? That's the tricky point here, making sure that your source knows what you can do and represents you accurately and completely without losing the game for you in a shortsighted sales pitch on your behalf. Write it out for them to ensure that they get it right. Make it clear that you're not expecting a sale, at least not in the first meeting. What you want is a chance to open a relationship that might prove mutually beneficial but in which you're willing to give before you get.

Make a referral their suggestion. "If you know them well enough, could you tell me a little bit about them and how best to approach them?" Ask: "It sounds like you know them pretty well. Would you be comfortable doing an e-mail/lunch/voice mail introduction? If it would help, I can even e-mail to you some introductory language."

Once you've secured the "yes, I'll introduce you," it's time to delve a little deeper. You're looking for what sorts of triggers can set up the right conversations. Work with your connection to help validate and verify the intelligence you need to open doors. Is there a particular issue that's of interest inside the doors of the company? Is there an issue that everyone ought to avoid discussing? Knowing what *not* to ask can be just as important as knowing what to ask.

ACCEPT

Graciously and generously accept help as it is offered. In *The Autobiography of Benjamin Franklin*, Franklin notes, "He that has once done you a kindness will be more ready to do you another, than he whom you yourself have obliged." Franklin discovered that sometimes it's better to get before you give. Psychologists call this, appropriately, the Ben Franklin effect.

People who have done you a favor are more likely to do another for you than they would be if they had received a favor from you. They like you better when they've done you a favor.

Why? Maybe because we feel better about ourselves when we are needed and viewed by others as having value to share. Accepting help is an act of generosity by you to others. If you think this is ridiculous, consider how you feel when a close friend is in a jam but doesn't turn to you for help. You may feel slighted. Thus, if you are still worried about how asking someone for referral assistance will affect your relationship, set that fear aside. When someone asks, "How can I be of help to you?" don't think too hard about it; tell that person how!

THANK

Demonstrate gratitude to your referral source before, during, and after the introduction is made. Once an introductory meeting has taken place on the basis of your friend's referral, immediately and specifically let your friend know and thank him or her regardless of the meeting's outcome. If it was a significant enough introduction, consider sending a handwritten note or even a gift of appreciation. Provide ongoing relationship feedback (if your referral source is comfortable with that) and ask for additional guidance on the relationship if you think it will be helpful. If the introduction turns to business, friendship, or anything else of positive value to you, show your referral source that you won't forget and explicitly give that person long-term credit for his or her kindness. Oh, and regardless of what Ben Franklin had to say, return the favor.

The figure on the next page provides a summary of the elements you need to remember in having more of the right connections.

02 Right Connections

PRIORITIZE
- •••• Clients
- •••• Prospects
- •••• Prospect Executives

CULTIVATE
- •••• Increase Willingness and Ability to Help
- •••• Balance Loose and Formal Referral Sources

HARVEST
- •••• Introductions
- •••• Information
- •••• Insights

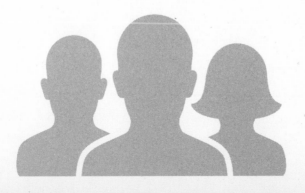

SECTION 4
RIGHT CONVERSATIONS: THE INFORMATION ADVANTAGE

RUN, PASS, KICK

15

Coach's Commentary

The difference between a tactic and a campaign is the difference between a single play on a football field and an entire season. Tactics are one-off, single-use methods; campaigns, in contrast, are systemic and ongoing. A campaign is a series of initiatives providing the venues for your consequential prospect conversations to take place. Campaigns are open-ended; tactics are closed-ended. Campaigns should always lead to consequential conversations.

OPENING

Right Connections + **Right Conversations** + Right Context

In pursuing your Opening Strategy, think campaigns, not tactics, and you'll be setting yourself up for a much longer, more fruitful run of openings. There are three tiers of campaigns in your Opening Playbook, and ideally, you'll deploy each of them at various times—or at the same time in varying intensities—to achieve your goals. The three tiers you'll employ are experiences, platforms, and programs.

All campaign tiers have the same basic objective, just as all seasons have the same number of games. They should be creating more of the right conversations with more of the right prospects with more of the right context and frequency. But it's what happens in a season of games—and within those campaigns—that requires finesse in matching campaigns with clients and prospects. Baseball coaches make decisions about batter-pitcher matchups every single inning of every game. Out in the bullpen, relief pitchers have certain tasks and abilities; some may be useful only against left-handed hitters, and others may be capable of throwing for several innings if the starter has trouble early. The idea, of course, is to match the right players with conditions, competitors, and game circumstances to gain advantage. In business development, you need to match the right campaign with the right prospect and situation.

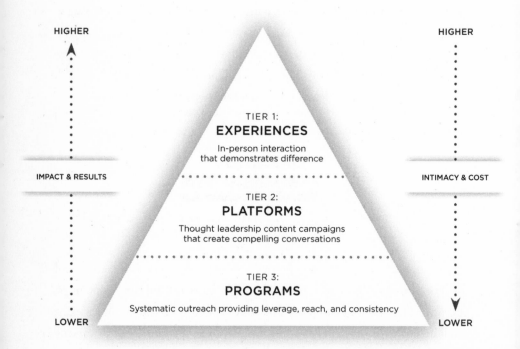

Let's delve deeper into these specific tiers.

TIER 1: EXPERIENCES

Provide a hands-on experience of what it is like to work with you and your firm. Candace's chocolate chip cookies provide a tangible (and delicious) look at what The Open Note has to offer its customers. From there, the door is open to greater experiences and a visceral understanding of what makes you different and better. Especially when you're selling the intangible, such as advisory services, the most persuasive tactics demonstrate exactly what it is like for a prospect to work with you.

Showing matters much more than telling. The goal is to lower your prospect's perceived risk of opening a relationship with you by letting the prospect try out the experience before you're officially hired.

Experiences that work best will demonstrate your capability and your likability as a professional and present significant value to your prospects even if they don't hire you on the spot. There are three potential objectives for an experience: (1) engagement—demonstrate what it's like to engage you, (2) entertainment—demonstrate likability by participating in a personally entertaining activity together, and (3) education—demonstrate your abilities as a thought partner for the prospect. In each case, the experience will allow you to have multiple in-person touch points and substantive conversations with the prospect over time.

Consider the following examples:

- **Engagement experience:** a small-scale, fixed-term project such as an assessment or audit of the prospect's current situation
- **Education experience:** a lunch-and-learn or webinar in which you educate the prospect's team on a current, critical issue at which you are an expert

- **Engagement experience:** examples of previous work products and deliverables (with appropriate protections of previous clients)

- **Engagement experience:** the way you conduct an initial problem-solving session with a prospect that demonstrates what it's like to work with you

- **Entertainment experience:** an annual event such as a wine tasting, skeet shooting, junket to the Masters golf tournament, dinner at your home, or any number of other creative encounters that you can create for a select set of your clients and prospects

Depending on your situation and your client's willingness to participate, you may or may not be able to offer engagement experiences free of charge, but you want to offer them at the least possible risk to your potential client. I'm not suggesting that you give your services away for free. Sampling doesn't necessarily require that. You should definitely articulate to your prospect the market rate for that work. Preferably, you will charge for it, because when prospects pay even a nominal fee for service, they're naturally more vested in it and the results. Even if you decide to waive your standard fee to deliver a trial-size version of your services, your prospect must understand that the expertise you deliver has significant value for which you typically get paid. A hybrid approach is to set a standard market value for the sample set of services you provide but offer to discount the cost of those services and roll that cost into the fee for a full engagement if the prospect decides to move forward with you after the sample or pilot.

Thought leadership initiatives that involve your prospect in the content's creation are another way to demonstrate what it is like to work with you. If you, for instance, include a prospect on a panel discussion that you moderate for a relevant audience, the prospect will learn how well organized you are (or not) and also experience what it's like to have you as a thought partner on the topics discussed.

Before offering or delivering a sample experience of your services, consider the best possible outcome. What happens if it goes well? Build in from the beginning a natural progression from the trial or test of your services to a fuller-scale engagement if the client is pleased with the test results.

A caution: delivering quality sample-size experiences may require you to spend significant amounts of time in customized, in-person prospect encounters. The intimacy of communication and impact tends to be very high, but so is the relative cost. As these experiences require one-to-one interaction with a specific prospect on a relevant business matter, there are only so many of them that you can pursue. Experiences deliver high value for your prospect and for you, but they aren't usually very scalable. Although they are powerful, sampling experiences alone are not enough. That brings us to the next tactic.

TIER 2: PLATFORMS

There are two important elements to a business development platform that opens the right conversations with prospects: the substance and the delivery mechanism.

Substance

The substance of a business development platform is a strong point of view— or claim to fame—expressed through thought leadership content. In politics, a platform refers to the declared set of policies and principles to which a candidate or party commits. In business development, one way to describe a platform is as a set of policies and principles related to one's area of expertise that are expressed through writing, speaking, and other thought leadership endeavors. For instance, a professional developing a platform on fair value measurement would note that she's written two books on the topic and is the keynote speaker at the upcoming American Institute of Certified Public Accountants fair market value conference.

How do you create substantive thought leadership? Anticipate the next big thing; don't just review history. Content that anticipates the needs and issues that your clients and prospects face is a powerful way to break through the incessant thought leadership noise. One way to accomplish this kind of visionary thought leadership is to study the general market forces and trends in your prospects' sector and envision the direct, ground-level implications. Play the "what if?" game: What would have to happen in the industry for the future to unfold in the ways you imagine? Put yourself in your clients' shoes and consider the types of decisions that they will have to make in regard to a specific trend. Develop several scenarios related to the trend and decision outcomes. Brainstorm the business opportunities inherent in the future scenarios. You don't have to present the answer—you're not pretending to be Nostradamus, after all, and you don't want to be too wrong—you just have to map out a framework that helps your clients and prospects consider what may come next. The more you involve your prospects and clients in these thought experiments, the more you turn them into relationship-building collaborations: thought partnership.

If you can't anticipate or be first to write or speak about a new trend, you may be able to see old trends in a new way. Counterintuitive approaches to issues in your field are especially good ways to gain attention for your writing or speaking material. The questions you ask yourself are the ones that yield these provocative content angles. Consider a standard, obvious, even "sacred" issue in your field. What if you reversed the assumptions related to this issue? What if you argued for the opposite of the conventional wisdom? Innovation often occurs this way. For instance, Henry Ford reversed the usual manufacturing question of his day: "How can we get the workers to the material?" Instead, he asked, "How can we get the material to the workers?" From there, the assembly line was created.

Many professionals are daunted by the concept of thought leadership, imagining that they must produce lavish reports, splendid oratory, Pulitzer Prize–winning books, or a major research piece involving hundreds of labor-hours of development, data collection, and analysis. Paralyzed by fear of failure, some professionals instead do nothing.

Think again. Useful thought leadership can be something much simpler and more basic than an idea that shakes your industry to its foundations. Start small. Be specific. Pick a subject or angle you can be famous for, one that matches your Opening Strategy. Make sure the approach you take fits your natural skills and abilities as an advisor. If you're a born thought leader, that's great. Research, write, speak. But if you're a natural connector, consider hosting a roundtable discussion in which you can show off your ability to connect people and ideas. If you're a driver, consider developing a system for regularly sending out books, articles, and newsletters written by others but relevant to your prospects. Think of thought leadership as more than just a branding opportunity; think of it as a chance for direct and meaningful dialogue with your best clients and prospects.

Let's narrow down the steps to providing first-rate thought leadership that serves business development purposes. These are the ways in which you can make this tactic work for you over and over before, during, and after each thought leadership initiative:

- **Step 1.** Before you begin writing or speak at an event, how can you include clients and prospects in your preparation efforts? Can you ask their views of the issue on which you will write or speak? What else can you do *before you start the ball rolling*?

- **Step 2.** When you write the article or speak at the event, how can you include clients and prospects in your material? Can you quote them? Can you include them on a panel? What else can you do *during* the thought leadership activity that will maximize your exposure and dialogue?

- **Step 3.** After the article is published or the event occurs, how will you follow up with attendees and nonattendees? Will you send a summary of the talk? Will you send a copy of the article with a letter indicating your latest thoughts or feedback you've received? How else can you follow up *after* the activity?

- **Step 4.** If you've completed steps 1 through 3, have you earned the right to present a *sample-size experience* of your services to the thought leadership audience? Connect the thought leadership material with an unmet need of your clients and prospects and show them how you can help.

Delivery Mechanism

If the first element of a successful business development platform is finding provocative content that engages your prospects and clients of choice, the second is developing a repeatable method for sharing your primary aims, principles, opinions, and expertise with the right people at the right time. A platform is the method, program, or initiative that allows your thought leadership to reach large numbers of the right connections in a consistent, systematic, and intentional manner. Your efforts to create thought leadership may often be thwarted by your standing client commitments. Employing the right self-sustaining, self-perpetuating mechanism can keep your marketing moving forward on other fronts even while you are deep in the weeds servicing existing clients.

The best marketing/business development platforms are thought leadership programs that serve multiple purposes. A first-rate platform mechanism does the following:

- Amplifies and enhances your thought leadership message

- Showcases and reinforces your claim to fame or Opening Strategy

- Provides a consistent means by which you connect with your existing and potential clients

- Allows you to "sell without selling," putting you in direct, meaningful conversation with your best clients and prospects

- Establishes you as a thought partner and peer of your prospects, not as a transactional peddler residing far down the industry food chain

- Can be highly leveraged, allowing you to reach more people at the same time relative to the more one-to-one nature of sampling experiences

- Self-generates additional content that you can use for future business development purposes

- Can be scheduled and repeated on a regular basis so that you are "pulled" into consistent business development

Platforms are as broad as your imagination as long as they embody these characteristics. Consider the following examples of quality platforms that serve both clients and creators:

- **Peer-to-peer roundtables.** Based on your positioning, these are especially good because they are easy and inexpensive to execute and provide an intimate, low-pressure environment to build relationships. Participants like these types of sessions because they are conversational and participatory, giving them the opportunity to make important industry and career contacts. One useful example is the CFO round table program launched by one of the world's largest commercial real estate services firms. They conduct quarterly programs in select U.S. cities at which chief financial officers from leading companies meet in an unfettered peer-to-peer learning and networking environment. As a result of these events, the real estate firm brokers who facilitate the events gain unprecedented access to CFOs in a way that their competitors cannot match.

- **Survey initiatives** or, even better, surveys that lead to rankings. These allow you and your professional colleagues to interview prospects in person and provide multiple touch points for you to build relationships that sell. For instance, a regional accounting firm cocreated and executes a fast-growing middle-market company ranking for key markets in their region. CFOs and CEOs of midsize companies that are interested in participating must be interviewed and have their financials validated by the CPA firm's partners to be eligible for inclusion.

- **Awards programs.** Everyone likes being given an award, right? Creating awards programs that allow participants a share of glory they can take back to their superiors are a win-win for everyone involved. For instance, Creative Growth Group runs an annual program that recognizes the select professional services firms that delivered the most compelling client experience over the last 12 months. These Advisors of Choice are matched by another tier of award winners—Clients of Choice—who demonstrated their commitment to ensuring that the professional services firms they engaged over the last 12 months were fully equipped to deliver optimal results for their company.

- **Blogs and podcasts.** Especially when the content is interview-centric, this type of platform allows you to get in front of prospects and help them look good to the public at large. A rising-star commercial real estate broker who serves creative class companies created a unique blog and event series that puts him at peer level with his city's entrepreneurial leadership. For these types of companies—as Candace clearly understands—workspace is an important tool to attract and retain the best workforce. In this broker's blog, he video interviews the CEOs of fast-growth ventures and also captures their ultracool office spaces on film and puts it all on the web. The site and the event series have opened myriad doors for him to his town's creative class leadership, who now turn to him for office space expertise.

Your platform doesn't have to be one of these types. What it does need to be is consistent, sustainable, and accessible. It also needs to be appropriately crafted to maximize the number of touch points you have with prospects before, during, and after each platform event.

The point is this: it is extremely beneficial to have a mechanism that brings your claim to fame to life and sets up more opportunities for you to have substantive conversations with the right prospects.

Now you have your thought leadership and your platform well under way. Outstanding. But how do you remind prospects that you exist even when you are buried deep in client work or busy executing experiences and platforms? You need to have some activities that keep working on your behalf even while you sleep.

TIER 3: PROGRAMS

Programs are low-touch, high-leverage campaigns that allow you to maintain a virtual conversation with many others without your being there. These are primarily digital/online activities using tools such as social media, e-mail, blogs, webinars, and digital content marketing. Although these initiatives are most typically used to raise brand awareness for a professional or his or her firm, our interest is in their power to open relationships and opportunities and keep them open in a scalable manner. The relatively low cost of content delivery and the always-on access afforded by online and mobile technologies make it possible to conduct methodical, systematic, scheduled outreach. They also allow your prospects to respond to you—engage in virtual dialogue—at a time and place that suits them.

Here are some examples:

Podcasts. Business creativity guru Todd Henry is now a bestselling author with a thriving consulting practice. His success originated with a podcast—*The Accidental Creative*—in which he interviewed other bestselling authors, expert consultants, and creativity gurus.

Social networks. Twitter, Facebook, and LinkedIn are among the myriad social network distribution channels for scheduling and posting a stream of content that can engage new and existing relationships. Tools to support those tools, such as TweetDeck, also exist to schedule content through many such channels at times of your choosing. Beware, though, of scheduling tweets that seem inauthentic or spammy; social media users are among the most astute people in the world and will be able to sniff out content that seems robotic or generic.

Blogs/e-newsletters. My firm uses a combination of a simple, ubiquitous web content tool to manage our blog—www.growing professionalservices.net—and a simple, ubiquitous e-mail newsletter tool to pull clients and prospects to it. If I can do it, you can.

What turns a digital branding activity into a business development dialogue? It is the way you balance listening and asserting a point of view. Since dialogue inherently involves two-way communication, digital business development programs that simply spurt your limited views close the door to conversation. An in-person conversation consists of listening and asserting, and so should your digital dialogues. Through your digital content, show your prospects and clients how you are interacting with them, hearing their opinions, feeling their pain, and welcoming their contribution.

Certainly, you want to stimulate readers to comment on your online assertions, hypotheses, and observations. Another way to include your prospects' voices is to interview them and include them in the original content. Yet another is to hand the microphone to them, allowing them to provide a guest submission to your online forum. Some tools, such as LinkedIn Groups, combine all these elements. You don't always need to be the author. You can programmatically facilitate and orchestrate content contributions from others and discussions across many participants and links to other people's content.

The purpose of a digital business development program is not to eliminate your presence in opening relationships. It is to help you have a conversational presence without the intensity and cost demanded by high-touch, in-person encounters.

MATCHING CAMPAIGNS TO PROSPECTS

Ideally, you will utilize all three of the campaign tiers, though not all tiers should be used for all prospects. Reserve your higher-cost, higher-touch campaigns for your highest-potential prospects and highest-value clients. Stay in touch with your longer-term prospects by using your lower-cost-per-contact, lower-touch campaigns:

Tier 1. Experiences should be reserved for your gold and blue tiers: your elite clients of choice and your elite, high-probability prospects.

Tier 2. Platforms should be shared with your gold and blue tiers, and you should also add your high-expected-value, longer-time-to-payoff prospects to the invitation list.

Tier 3. Programs are for all of your contacts: gold, blue, red, and orange. They allow you to stay in front of those with whom you can't spend in-person time and reinforce your credibility with those whom you are courting more directly.

Campaigns are the umbrella initiatives and venues where meaningful conversations take place. But what does a meaningful conversation look like? Read on.

CALL THE RIGHT PLAY ◼ **16**

Roll Game Film

The next day, Allen made a few calls on behalf of Sam and Becca. Without exception, his contacts were surprisingly warm and receptive to the idea of helping out a friend of Allen's. Also without exception, they were a bit surprised to hear from Allen. Indeed, he heard "How long has it been since we talked?" so often that he started to realize he needed to do a far better and more frequent job of talking to people. Also, the fact that so many people related to him in a purely social manner—there was little talk of his work but plenty about his wife, his kids, and upcoming cookouts—told him he needed to do a far better job of reminding people of what he actually did for a living. Weekend parties and golf outings were fine in and of themselves, but he needed to be doing more with the benefits he'd been given.

Allen realized a sobering fact. He'd privately scoffed at Becca's lack of drive in getting ahead but understood now that he had a similar problem: he hadn't done nearly enough with his contact list to start and maintain the kinds of conversations he needed to take his own steps forward. Knowing people was wonderful; making sure they knew what you could do for them was invaluable.

Candace brought this message home to him a few days later when he stopped in to pick up some cupcakes for a function at his kids' school. "You want to know something strange, Allen? I don't drink coffee."

"You don't drink coffee? Really? But you run a coffee shop!"

"I know. Doesn't quite seem to mesh, does it? But here's the truth: the coffee is just a vehicle. It's not really what I'm selling. It's a conversation starter, a way to get the ball rolling. I found that people are more relaxed over coffee than they are in an office. Same thing with a golf course, a grill, a football game; whatever medium you want to use, you'll find people are more than willing to talk with you if they've got that kind of social entrée to smooth the way. The task for you," she said, handing him the cupcakes, "is to figure out how to take that next step and get people talking about more than just the ball game or what's on the grill. Once you do that, you're golden."

"Look, Candace, I'll let you in on a secret," Allen said. "The truth is that I have always had trouble making that leap. I've got no problem with the chitchat; I know enough about everyone in my contact list to keep a nice steady flow of conversation going along the surface. But then, when the time comes to get to it, I never quite know what to say to bridge that gap. It always comes across as forced."

"That makes a lot of sense, and I understand where you're coming from," Candace said. "Let's kick it around with Sam and Becca. I've got a few ideas you might want to consider."

Becca showed up promptly at noon, as she'd always done, and Sam wandered in a few minutes later, stuffing his phone into his pocket as he came in the door. Candace motioned them over to Allen's table. After a bit of introductory how-have-you-been small talk, Candace leaned forward.

"Well, I suppose you're wondering why I've called you here today," she said to a laugh, and she nodded at Allen. "That's one way to do it, smoothing the transition with a little humor." Allen nodded back in understanding.

"The topic of the day is communication," Candace said, "specifically the kinds of conversations that bring value to those around you. All three of you are wonderful and delightful people, but nobody's really much interested in that when they're considering whether you can make them more money. And while that's an awfully mercenary way to look at conversations, sometimes it's helpful to boil it down to those bare, essential elements: What is each one of us getting out of this conversation?"

She continued. "A couple weeks back, you wouldn't believe who walked in that door," she said, motioning toward the front of the café. She mentioned the name of a movie star so huge that all three of them turned around to look with new eyes at The Open Note. He was in here? Really?

"And you're just telling us about this now?" Sam said. "I'd be trumpeting that all over the city!"

"Well, make no mistake, I did drop a little tip to the paper's gossip editor, and we got a nice write-up there," Candace said. "But that's not really what I'm looking for out of The Open Note. I don't want this to become some kind of celebrity-stalking hangout. Plus," she added with a sly grin, "he told me he liked how calm it was here . . . and that he'd be back."

They all laughed then, giving Candace a bit of grief and hinting that she should just pitch this whole coffee shop thing and go be a Hollywood wife. She waved it off and tried to redirect the conversation.

"Stop, stop!" she said. "You're missing the whole point. The whole time Mr. Hollywood Big Shot was here—sat right there in that chair—three or four people came up and tried to talk to him. And while he was very gracious, the conversations all went the same way: 'I love your movies, you're so awesome . . . bye!'"

"As opposed to you, who was so calm and collected," Sam said.

"Quiet, you. No, the point here is this: the conversation was completely unbalanced. Mr. Movie Star had plenty to offer the fans—the aura of celebrity, a bit of reflected glory, that kind of thing. But they didn't have anything to offer him other than praise, which, you know, he probably gets an awful lot. For a conversation to survive past the how-have-you-been stage—this is what we've been talking about, Allen—you have to offer more. You have to bring some elements to the table that the other party can't get anywhere else, or can't get anywhere else at that moment."

Candace looked at Sam. "Mind if I use you as an example again?"

Sam held his arms wide. "Why not? My skin is as thick as asphalt at this point."

"You know the story about Sam's client meeting of a few weeks back, the one where he nearly got thrown out of the office." Becca and Allen nodded in sympathy.

"Anyway, Sam made a few mistakes there—it's okay, Sam, everybody makes a mistake once; the trick is not making them again. Sam's major mistake was this: he had the right contact, the exact man who could have given him more business, who could have opened doors for him. But Sam engaged in the wrong conversation, focusing on movies and other rabbit holes and then leaping straight into please-please-hire-me. Not a whole lot of grace in that, and you can see why he didn't get very far."

"You make it sound like every conversation is a performance, an audition," Becca said. "That sounds like a lot of pressure."

"Does it?" Candace said. "I guess you could look at it that way. It's really a way of just breaking down what we all know from kindergarten." She pulled out her tablet and began swiping at it with her finger. "We don't write on napkins here." She smiled.

"Now, this is what we're talking about," she said, and on the tablet she'd written:

CONVERSATIONS

1.

2.

3.

"Class is in session," Allen said.

"Indeed," Candace replied, "so pay attention. There are three ways to get a conversation to rise up above the normal back-and-forth of our day-to-day life. Any thoughts on what one might be?"

"You've got to have something worth saying," Sam said.

"Exactly," Candace said. "We are all special and precious flowers, but we don't always have that much that's interesting to say. Despite what Twitter and Facebook and the rest of the more social of the social networks would have you believe, I'm not always interested in hearing about your meals or your political views or your kids. Great for you, not so great for me. Bring me something that engages me." And she wrote:

CONVERSATIONS

1. CONTENT

2.

3.

"A quality conversation has to have content to it. Something of substance to the other person, preferably. There has to be some meat on the bone there. What else?"

"You've got to be interested in what the other person is saying," Allen said. "Even if they've got some great 'content' to offer, if they're not doing it in an interesting way, you don't really care about it."

"Yes," Candace said. "You've got to be interesting and bring content of interest. That's true. I know that the ebbs and flows of the financial market are interesting and necessary, but I have no understanding of how they actually impact me on anything more than a very basic level. So if somebody was going to come in here and give me a lecture on derivatives, my eyes would glaze over before they got to the end of their first sentence. Each speaker needs to engage the other's . . ."

CONVERSATIONS

1. CONTENT

2. CURIOSITY

3.

"Curiosity. Allen, you described one important component of curiosity: offer something interesting to the other party, not just to yourself," Candace continued. "But what is it that is most interesting to others no matter who they are?"

"Money," Allen said.

"Sex," Sam said.

"Rock 'n' roll?" Becca laughed.

"Themselves," Candace said.

> "You become much more interesting to others when you demonstrate how interested you are in them. Before each key conversation you have with prospects, consider what it is that makes you most curious about them, their organization, and the challenges and opportunities they face."

"When your conversation is under way and you've had your initial curiosity quenched, then pay attention to the questions that come to mind next and pursue that fresh curiosity. I'm not talking about phony curiosity—asking questions just to pretend you care and then ignoring the answers. I'm not talking about manipulative curiosity—proceeding to interrogate your prospects, with a formulaic set of questions designed to entrap them. I'm talking about a heartfelt interest in them and their success. If you can't feel that, it's fair to question why you're in the conversation at all.

"And that brings us to the third element of a successful conversation, which, as you can probably guess, begins with a *C*. Any ideas?"

The table was quiet for a moment, and then the suggestions flowed fast and furious.

"Coffee?"

"Coins?"

"Captivity?"

"Cheese?"

"No, no, no," Candace said, waving off all the suggestions. "Good ideas, but—" She paused. "Cheese? Really, Sam." He shrugged.

"You're hopeless. Anyway, the third element of a good conversation is what you three were just doing . . . or trying to do, anyway."

CONVERSATIONS

1. CONTENT

2. CURIOSITY

3. COLLABORATION

"There it is. A conversation isn't one person spouting off at another; that's a lecture or a soliloquy."

A conversation involves both people collaborating to find a higher level that neither one could have reached on his or her own.

"Maybe that's something as simple as finding a new book to read, and maybe it's something as far-reaching as an eventual marriage. You never know."

"It makes a lot of sense, laid out like that," Allen said. "Each one builds on the other."

"Exactly," Candace said. "Look, I know we're making the art of conversation sound like rocket science or something, but it's really a matter of focusing and paying attention to what's around you. You would be amazed at how many people fail in the simple task of just paying attention to someone other than themselves."

"So what's our task, teach?" Sam said. "And do we get free lunch this time?"

"This one's homework," Candace said. "Pay very close attention to what's asked of you here in this scenario. It's not just about listening to what the other person says. It's about you having something to offer as well. You don't want to be the starstruck fan gawking open-mouthed at the celebrity. You want to engage that movie star in a conversation. It's doable. It happens all the time. And it's now your task: figure out what it is that you have to offer a potential contact. Allen, what do you have to offer in a conversation?"

"Well, my firm has been ranked among the top—"

"BZZZZT!" Candace said, making a large X with her arms. "Wrong answer. It's not just about how great you are. They could learn that from a simple Google search. You're trying to demonstrate to people that you're more than just a walking brochure. So with that in mind, go forth, my students, and think about what you've got to offer in a conversational setting."

"Seems easy enough," Sam said.

"*Seems* being the operative word," Candace said. "I want you to use your conversational skills in a professional environment to break some new ground. Chat with a colleague to exchange new marketing techniques. Talk up a client to learn how others are handling technology in this new environment. Anything, anything at all, just as long as you actually do the work and report back here next week."

"Will the movie star be here?"

"You never know." Candace smiled. "But if he is, don't you want to be prepared?"

COMMAND THE HUDDLE

17

Coach's Commentary

Old-school selling techniques are filled with phrases like "getting a foot in the door." Think about what that means for a second. When do you have your foot in a door? When someone's trying to close it in your face and you're actively trying to prevent him or her from doing so (or, in extreme circumstances, when you've kicked through a door). This doesn't seem like the foundation of a winning partnership, does it? Instead, it sounds like the prelude to a call to security.

That's why we don't use the tired foot-in-the-door metaphor.

We want to take the door off its hinges. We don't want the door to exist in the first place.

The only way to remove that door is to make sure you orchestrate the right interactions, the right conversations, with your clients.

You've been having conversations all your life, but have you ever really thought about the components of a conversation? Let's break it down. You know that the basic interactions of a heart-to-heart with your parent and an eye-glazing soliloquy at a cocktail party are the same, but the two conversations couldn't be more different.

There are three primary elements of a good, productive, interesting conversation:

Content of consequential value to the other person

Curiosity about the other person that is authentic and attentive

Collaboration that positions you on the same side of the table with your conversational partner

For our purposes, this is a prospect with whom you can cocreate solutions, moving forward toward the next conversation.

It's likely that you've never taken a close look at conversational dynamics before, but then, why would you? We've been having conversations our entire lives. It's not second nature; it's fifth or sixth nature. But if you think about it, every good conversation you've ever had has included those three elements and every bad conversation has lacked one or all of them. Let's dig deeper.

CONTENT

To connect with content means to improve your rapport with a prospect by consistently bringing something of consequential value to the prospect's organization, the prospect's career, or the prospect personally.

Remember how Candace said that great conversations aren't rocket science? Well, maybe they aren't, but consider for a minute the theory of the expanding universe espoused by some physicists. Is it right? Who knows? More recently, other physicists have suggested that the universe may be shrinking. No matter. What we need you to do is expand your mind when it comes to content. We need a Big Bang to take place in your brain when it comes to the multitude of ways you can bring value to your prospects without giving away the galaxy before you're hired. Before we blow out your thinking about what content is, let's explode and evaporate the things that content isn't.

We need to blow up your misguided views of content like a box of
Acme Corporation dynamite on Wile E. Coyote.

No, this *isn't* content:

Solicitation. Asking a prospect for his or her business before the time is right is not content. It is solicitation. Handing your firm's brochure to your prospect or a pitch book or anything else that lists your credentials is not content. It is solicitation material. There may be a time and place for those things, but don't fool yourself into thinking they are valuable to your prospect. They're valuable to you. That's not content for the purposes of opening a relationship.

Self-praise. Articles featuring your firm that are heralded on the cover of some hack magazine where you paid to get editorial coverage is not content. Press releases about your firm are not content. Tombstone ads announcing your latest successful deals are not content. They're not bad things and there's a time and place for them, but if you think they're of value to your client, snap out of it!

Shiny objects. Pens, mugs, hats, shirts, and any other bric-a-brac with your firm's logo on them are not. They are tchotchkes. Holiday cards and gifts are not content. They're shiny objects. They're nice and fun and make about a millisecond of a branding impact, but surely you don't believe they're substantive content. Right?

> Think of solicitation, self-praise, and shiny objects not as content but
> as a loss, a theft, or a penalty imposed by you on your prospect.

They do your prospects no good and in fact steal valuable time from them or clutter their lives. They earn you this type of reaction when you call the next time: "Oh, jeez, it's that Sam guy calling again. I need to remember to block his number."

Yes, this *is* content:

Insights. Too often, too many people view content solely as thought leadership: writing, speaking, research. Others may think first of the content marketing trend soaking up budgets, which almost always implies offering thought leadership materials online as a way to drive prospects to a firm's website. Those things are great and helpful, but those limited definitions focus on substantive information as the full extent of content.

Providing thought leadership information doesn't necessarily equate to sharing insight or implications that an audience can use. Turning information into unique insights and powerful implications that your prospects couldn't have gotten any other way—and helping your audience take action on the basis of those things—now, that's content!

Introductions. Remember that we are defining content as something of consequential value to your prospect's organization or career or to the prospect personally. Thus, content includes connecting a prospect to an appropriate person from your inventory of relationships, someone with whom the prospect can prosper personally and professionally. If you do this before you're commercially engaged by a prospect without any quid-pro-quo expectation, that's definitely content. Just the right contact can affect your prospect's organization—say, the perfect candidate for a position that's hard to fill. Just the right connection can influence your prospect's career—perhaps an experienced executive who has held a similar role and can serve as a mentor to the prospect. Just the right introduction can make a personal difference, too—making life easier or better for your prospect or his or her family.

Income. There's no denying that money is of consequential value to us all. If you are able to connect your prospect to a new customer for her organization's products or services, that counts as content in our expansive definition. If you are able to connect a prospect to a recruiter who lands him a paid gig on the board of directors of a thriving company, that counts as content. Net income is the excess of revenue over expenses, so if before you are officially engaged to help you can save your prospect money, that's content too.

> Think of insights, introductions, and income as content
> gifts that support the prospect's success.

Content earns you this type of response when you call the next time: "Oh, great! Sam is calling. Every time he reaches out, something good happens. I learn something I needed to know. I meet someone who can help me. I get a new piece of business. Hey, Sam, how ya doin'?"

Reconsider Sam's encounter with Joe Jordan. The only information Sam brought to the meeting was about his own capabilities. Did Jordan need to spend his time hearing that? How did it leave Jordan better off for having met with Sam? He didn't and he wasn't, and as a result Sam got shown both the proverbial and the literal door. There was no chance for Sam to take this particular door off its hinges.

Every conversation, every interaction, has to bring at least some content of value to each party for there to be any kind of incentive to seek out the next conversation. Here are some examples of how you might provide insights, introductions, or income to support the success of your prospect's organization, career, or personal circumstances.

CONNECT WITH CONTENT*

Content is not just information; it is anything of value to the other person

	INSIGHTS	INTRODUCTIONS	INCOME
ORGANIZATIONAL	"Here's an article, white paper, research study, etc. that may be of help to your organization" Or "I was thinking about what your company is trying to accomplish and wondered what would happen if you tried XYZ."	"May I introduce you to a company that might be a good alliance for your organization?"	"Here's a lead (they actually need services like yours right now!) that might help your company."
PROFESSIONAL	"Here's an article, white paper, research study, etc. that may be relevant to your role." Or "I was thinking about what you are trying to get done and wondered what would happen if you tried XYZ."	"May I introduce you to a company that might be a good business contact for you in your career?"	"Here's a lead that might help you."
PERSONAL	"I know that you're really interested in XYZ hobby and thought this might be interesting to you (your kid, wife, friend, etc.)" Or "I was thinking about how you like to do XYZ and wondered if you ever…"	"May I introduce you to an individual who may share the same personal interests and be able to help you advance yours?"	"Here's someone who is looking to hire people just like you."

If content is a gift, you must present it appropriately wrapped: as a hypothesis, this insight, introduction, or income opportunity may be valuable to your prospect, but you want to get the prospect's view on it first. You have to deliver that content gift in an open-ended way, not with simple yes-or-no questions. Instead, ask *what*, ask *how*, ask *why*. Say, "I wonder if . . ." and engage the prospect in exploring the hypothesis with you. "I wonder if this person I know might be a good contact for you. What do you think?" These are the ways to keep conversations moving forward and open. Yes and no are conversational brick walls, forcing you to redirect to get around or over them. Look farther down the road; don't let yes or no stop you cold.

CURIOSITY

Let's be honest. If someone is discussing a topic with which you have particular affinity, whether business or personal, you're going to be dialed in, hanging on every word and ready to contribute your own perspective. But there will be times—many, many times—when you're speaking with a prospect with whom you have little affinity and who has little to discuss that's of immediate interest to you. That's when you need to spark your curiosity in what that person has to offer. Consider how Sam could have shown more curiosity in his early dealings, the way he could have shown interest in what Joe Jordan or others have to offer.

There's an acronym for sparking curiosity about what a prospect has to offer: DOTS. Keep the DOTS in mind—connect the dots, if you will—and you'll see possibilities open wide in conversation.

D: Distinctions. What makes this person and his or her organization unique? Every individual, every organization has its unique qualities. Observe what they are. Speak about them.

O: Opportunities. What does your prospect need to accomplish? What opportunities is he or she seeking, and in turn, how can you help the prospect maximize those opportunities?

T: Triggers. What affects your prospects' growth both internally and externally? What causes immediate changes in the prospects' environment, and how can you help them prepare and adjust for those changes?

S: Similarities. What do you have in common with this individual? Some affinities, such as age, geographic background, and industry are obvious. Others may take a bit more effort to discern. But the more you can find common ground, the stronger and more rewarding your conversations will be.

CONNECTING THE DOTS

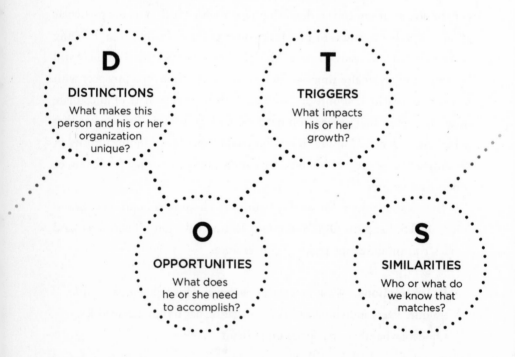

D

DISTINCTIONS

What makes this person and his or her organization unique?

T

TRIGGERS

What impacts his or her growth?

O

OPPORTUNITIES

What does he or she need to accomplish?

S

SIMILARITIES

Who or what do we know that matches?

COLLABORATION

Ever been in a conversation that wasn't a conversation but a one-sided lecture, a monologue about the speaker's exploits or worldview? You wanted to get out of that conversation as fast as humanly possible, didn't you? That's because the conversation wasn't anything approaching collaboration, an exchange of ideas rather than a river flowing one way.

A productive collaborative encounter involves a peer-to-peer exchange of ideas rather than a one-sided power struggle. By allowing your contacts to open up as colleagues, not as competitors, you gain the chance to better understand what value means to them and demonstrate your ability to deliver it. For his part, Sam missed the chance to engage his new relationship in thought partnership and in a cocreation of ideas and opportunities to add more value to the prospect's efforts.

Also, remember that you're not interrogating the prospect. You're not trying to trap or one-up that person. What you're trying to do is cocreate an understanding of the prospect's situation and together divine a path to its likely solution.

> One of the ways you can build trust is to demonstrate your commitment to truth, and one of the best ways to do that is to reveal it gently but directly.

To understand what this means, let's turn back to the gridiron. Football offenses use information and signals, communicated right up to the last instant before the ball is snapped, to describe the reality of their field position and call the appropriate play.

That information and signaling isn't held exclusively in one person's hands, however. The quarterback isn't the only offensive player on the field who will read the defense and select the play that is about to come. The center, the lineman who plays in the middle of the offensive line and who snaps the ball to begin play, often has a better view of the defensive formation than the quarterback does. In the moments before a snap, the defensive linemen will shift and slide, move up and retreat, point and shout, and generally do their best to disguise their intentions and confuse the offense. Meanwhile, the offensive line and the quarterback depend on the center to read the defense as it shifts position before the snap and to make line calls for the entire offense to follow. It is a give-and-take of information, a collaboration, that determines the best offensive action. The coach, the offensive coordinator, the quarterback, the center—all contribute on every play.

An opening encounter with a prospect is a similar situation. We need to be certain that both sides are sharing everything necessary to solve a problem; if a quarterback doesn't communicate a defensive shift to the line, he could end up on his back a few seconds later. Although a quarterback and his offense don't really have time to ask questions of each other, you and your prospect do. Don't let conversations proceed without inquiry and follow-up designed to bring you and your prospect closer in alignment. Take the time. Ask one more question. You'll be surprised where it could lead. Questions are the primary tool we have for eliciting essential hidden facts.

But it's not just about getting the prospect to open up. We need to make sure we do the same thing, disclosing what we know about the prospect's situation and industry to help the prospect make informed choices about the best way forward. It should go without saying that if a prospect later learns that we had information that could have helped him or her along the way, we've killed any chance of landing that prospect—and anyone that prospect knows—as a client.

There are also aspects of a situation that neither you nor your client knows. For instance, there may be activities taking place in the market or among competitors that no one in the conversation can discern. How do you proceed when neither of you possesses necessary information? The key, of course, is brainstorming and creating contingency plans. On every pass play, a quarterback has a checkdown receiver—someone who goes only a short distance down the field, enough to gain some small positive yardage. If every other option is covered, the quarterback checks down to this receiver, usually his third or fourth option. The receiver won't get much in the way of yardage, but it's better than taking a sack or throwing an interception.

The advisor who earns the trust of a prospect is the one who smoothly enables the flow of truth between himself or herself and the prospect so that all the information is available and signals are interpreted properly to provide a complete solution to or proposal for solving the prospect's problems.

It's important to remember that we're talking about collaborative problem solving here, unique solutions for unique problems. Collaborative problem solving is a function of training and education. We learn ways to think and approach problems differently, and we then practice those ways to benefit our business development efforts.

Forget any notion of trick plays—anything remotely smacking of sales manipulation—in your collaborative efforts. Authentic curiosity about your prospect's path to success combined with substantive content and customized collaboration is the key to creating conversations that lead to engagement and solutions. Genuinely seek to discuss the matters most immediately important to your contact regarding his or her company, career, or personal circumstances and you'll advance the ball.

The accompanying figure provides a summary of the elements you need to pursue the right conversations that open relationships and opportunities.

03   *Right Conversations*

CAMPAIGNS
- Experiences
- Platforms
- Programs

CONTENT
- Insights
- Introductions
- Income

CURIOSITY
- Distinctions
- Opportunities
- Triggers

COLLABORATION
- Similarities
- Cocreated
- Ideas Exchanged
- Truth Seeking

NO TRICK PLAYS

18

Roll Game Film

"It's strange," Sam was saying. "The fact that I'm paying more attention to my conversations now is really changing them. Taking a conversation apart lets you see how it all fits together, you know?"

Becca and Allen nodded. "I know we're supposed to be focused more on professional conversations, but I'm finding that I'm communicating better with everyone I meet," Allen said. "Friends, family, even the waiter at my table at dinner last night. My kids are falling all over each other to talk to me now. Well, OK, I may be exaggerating about that last part."

"Does it seem almost too easy to you, though?" Becca ventured. "I mean, talking to other people about what drives them is rewarding, at least for the other people, but when does it pay off for me? That's what I'm trying to figure out."

"I think it's a matter of having some faith," Sam said. "Enough of the right conversations at the right times with the right people leads to success, right, Candace?" She was orbiting around them, a blur of activity as the last of the morning rush was wrapping up.

"You got it, Sam," she said, not pausing in her work.

"I've got a fairly big lunch meeting coming up tomorrow," Sam said. "Possible client I've been trying to land for a while now. And I think I've got the perfect icebreaker line: 'What keeps you up at night?'"

Candace stopped in her tracks for a moment. Sam thought he read an expression of mild disgust on her face.

"That's a good one," Allen agreed.

"I can think of a few easy answers already," Becca added.

"Thanks!" Sam said. "My thinking is, this is the kind of line that you use in just about any situation. Everyone's got something that keeps them up at night, right? All I have to do is figure out what that is for each person, and from there I can figure out how to help them. Not bad, huh?"

"Simple. Effective," Allen said. "I've got one of my own: 'sharing our capabilities.' I work that phrase into a conversation somewhere along the way, and it opens all kinds of doors. Everyone likes to think they've got capabilities that can help someone else; this just plays on that."

Again Candace was close by, and hearing Allen's suggestion, she dropped some silverware accidentally and it clattered across the floor. When Sam looked, she was shaking her head vigorously—he figured it was because of the spill.

"Not bad," Sam said. "I might have to steal it."

"Just make sure we're not both talking to the same client." Allen laughed. "That could be awkward."

"How about you, Becca?" Sam said. "What's going to be your hook to get a conversation going?"

"Um . . . trick?" Becca said. "I'm not sure I actually have any sort of trick."

"And that's why Becca's the smartest of the three of you," Candace said, swooping past and pulling around a chair to join their circle.

"You were eavesdropping!" Sam said, mock horrified.

"It's my shop. That means it's not eavesdropping," Candace said smoothly. "Sorry for butting in, but I was hearing some things that were a little bit off base. Well, a little bit nauseating to tell you the truth."

"Really?" Sam said. "Did you hear my question, 'What keeps you up at night?'"

"Yes, that's exactly what I heard. That's exactly what I'm talking about. Didn't we talk about this? Remember, the trick here is that there is no trick. And a one-size-fits-all line like that is the very definition of a trick. Have you been reading through Roger's journals again?"

"But doesn't it get the conversation going?"

"Maybe. Or maybe it stops the conversation dead, because the person on the receiving end realizes it's basically the spoken version of a form letter. And when's the last time you spent a lot of time focused on what a form letter had to say?"

"'What keeps you up at night?' is one of those questions so trite that it usually brings responses like 'my dog' or 'my indigestion.'"

"But aren't we supposed to be getting them to talk about themselves, what they need?"

"Of course. But in a way that makes it seem like you're not reading off a menu of conversational options. Look, you're not just trying to get them to unload their problems. This isn't about finding your prospect's most exposed wound and jamming your thumb into it. You're not just looking to play doctor, therapist, or mechanic. You're looking to form a larger bond here, one that could be more lasting and have more than one use."

They nodded, and Candace continued. "Put yourself in the shoes of your conversational target. What do they want to get out of an interaction with you?"

"How are they going to be better off from having met with you?"

"To be flat-out honest, why should they take time out from their busy schedule to meet with you just to confess their problems to you?"

"How do you know what approach will work?" Allen said.

"That's the kind of answer you can only figure out in the context of the conversation itself," Candace said. "If you start trying to game that kind of thing ahead of time, you end up making a fool of yourself because you're like an actor trying to remember lines. Let the conversation breathe, remember."

"Candace," Becca said, seeing the frustration on her colleagues' faces, "when's a case when you had something like this? What did you do?"

Candace smiled. "See, that's a good question. Turn my wisdom around on me. Well done, Becca."

Allen and Sam nodded in understanding, and Candace looked up at the ceiling to think for a moment. Then she snapped her fingers.

"Got it," she said. "I've told you a little bit about what brought me into the coffee business, but I don't think I've ever told you about the financial side of it. A store like this doesn't just pop out of the ground, you know."

"It does if you're Starb—"

"Ah, ah, ah," Candace said. "Let's stay positive, shall we? Anyway, this is a perfect example of what I'm talking about. A few years after business school, while I was still toiling away working for other people, I was at a friend's surprise party. An old classmate of mine and I were talking, and although I'd known this guy for almost a decade, we'd never really talked business to any measurable degree. For whatever reason, this night our conversation turned to our professional aims.

"We started talking about our hopes and our regrets—not because of any kind of trigger question, just because the conversation flowed in that way naturally. And what he learned was that I had long nurtured a dream to create a place where people could one day come together to chat about everything in an environment that was every bit as homey as their own den."

"One of these days you'll get there," Sam said, sipping his coffee.

Candace smiled. "One of these days. Anyway, as it turns out, my friend had done quite a bit better than I had financially, and he offered to put up the seed capital to get me going. He connected me with a friend who ran a cupcake shop to give me a sense of the basics. That friend then connected me with a real estate broker who had a good sense of what properties were coming onto the market in the most viable locations for one of these sorts of shops. Distributors, advertising, attorneys . . . they all followed through word of mouth, one after the other. And I bet if you think hard enough, you can trace back how your own professional status came about as a result of a couple of well-timed conversations with the right people."

They did, and sure enough, each one of them could see how a chance call, a well-timed meeting, or a proper connection had brought them so much advantage in their lives.

"The reason that works so well," Candace said, "is that you've already established a bond of trust as personal friends that allows you to easily make the leap to business colleagues. It's a little easier doing it that way than the reverse, but the same principles apply: understand what to talk about and when to talk about it. Pretty easy, right?"

With that, Candace left them to attend to the afternoon's business. They had plenty to consider and not a whole lot of time to do it before their next round of hopefully productive conversations.

SECTION 5
RIGHT CONTEXT: THE EXPERIENCE ADVANTAGE

SHOW YOUR SKILLS

19

Coach's Commentary

What if a football team from Florida that wins every game it plays in the blazing rays of the Panhandle sun suddenly has to play in Wisconsin during the first ice storm of the season? Would you bet on that team to win? Even if you have the right team or athlete, you may have the wrong context for optimal performance. This is also true in business development. Context matters.

OPENING

Right Connections + Right Conversations + **Right Context**

Contextually appropriate conversations match the message with the situation. What if you select the right meeting location, appropriate content, and food-free collateral materials but you repeatedly call the prospect to arrange the meeting during the exact week in which his wife has asked for a divorce? How's that going to work out for you?

Context is the total set of circumstances that surround and influence your most consequential conversation.

It's the where, how, and when choices you make that demonstrate what makes you the right choice for a prospect. It is how you show your expert skills, advisory style, and caliber of service before you are bought. Context is the advantage you get by creating a phenomenal prospect experience.

Presenting yourself and your practice in a contextually appropriate way is a prospect-specific proposition. It means using your knowledge of a particular prospect's interests, needs, and preferences to provide that person with pinpoint relevant ideas and insights in a highly personalized and customized manner. The tone, truthfulness, and timing of the signals we send set the context of our opening encounters.

Signals are tangible manifestations of the otherwise unseen qualities that make us a good selection for our prospects of choice. The venue we choose, the way in which our presentation is designed, our attire, the car we drive, our educational pedigree, our social circle, and our overall executive presence signal our likability, capability, and credibility.

Whatever your prospect's needs, your job isn't to fake through artificial signals that you're a fit. It is instead to ensure that you truly are a fit and then provide signals that bring to life your true strengths. Manipulative closing is fauxthenticity. Authentic opening is being just what you are and putting yourself more frequently in front of those who value that. In the same way, authentic signaling is simply bringing to light the important elements that might otherwise be lost or unseen by your prospects and that indicate that they will get their needs met.

It's also worth noting that authentic doesn't necessarily mean perfect. Perfect can be intimidating and off-putting. Consider how uneasy you might feel in the presence of someone better-looking, more accomplished, more polished, and more knowledgeable than yourself. We're not suggesting that you dumb yourself down or ugly yourself up; by all means, highlight your highlights. But there's a difference between cool confidence and flaunting, just as there's a difference between approachable and pristine.

There are no straight lines in nature, and drawing a truly perfect circle is extraordinarily difficult. A little bit of imperfection is more honest, more truthful. The Japanese concept of *wabi-sabi* embodies this: the idea that imperfection is not just acceptable but desirable. Approach others as a human being, not as a straight-from-a-business-seminar model.

Remember how Candace brings warm cookies to new customers, especially those who seem like they could use a friendly touch. That helped create the context for her first open dialogue with Sam. Although Candace trains her café team members to pass the cookie plate only out of genuine, authentic care and interest, it is not an unintentional activity. She's discovered that three good things happen: (1) Her new customers get a visceral sample of Open Note service and a taste of its delicious baked goods, (2) the customer's first impression is of a positive, welcoming environment, and (3) the timing of the gesture is especially appreciated and trust building—healing, really—if the server accurately recognized the customer's blues. Candace doesn't just tell new customers what it's like to be a regular guest at The Open Note; she shows them.

Ignoring situational context is a recipe for business development disaster. Instead, you want to be mindful of context and arrange circumstances that strengthen rapport, enhance credibility, and showcase your unique claim to fame. That's the right context: the circumstances and settings that enable your most productive prospect interactions. Contextually appropriate circumstances and signals are defined by three elements: the right tone, truth, and timing:

- **Tone** defines how you secure and engage those conversations.

- **Truth** is delivering each prospect experience with authenticity and congruence.

- **Timing** is when and how often you reach out and touch your best prospects.

We'll see Candace's use of tone and truth in Chapter 20 and provide you with tools to follow her lead in Chapter 21. In Chapter 22, you'll see what Roger Smith has to say about timing and urgency and how Sam, Candace, and their cohorts go about it somewhat differently. In Chapter 23, you'll get this coach's analysis and recommendations regarding the ineffable issue of timing. For now, though, get out on the field and play ball. See for yourself how context can stall or accelerate your opening efforts.

YOUR PROSPECTS AREN'T THE OPPOSING DEFENSE

20

Roll Game Film

They sat in one of The Open Note's conference rooms, the one named "Harmony," and stared at the whiteboard. The completely blank whiteboard. None of them spoke.

Oh, they knew what they were supposed to be doing, of course. They knew they were supposed to be coming up with ways in which context could be leveraged to improve contact, ways they could step outside their traditional realms of experience to turbocharge their connections and forge deeper, more lasting connections. It was a great idea in theory. But in practice? They hadn't even figured out how to put it on the whiteboard.

"All right, I'll take the first hit," Sam said, standing up to write on the board. "This is pretty much how we handle all of our client contacts." He scrawled out a few quick lines:

1. See client

2. Make contact (and do that conversation stuff Candace talked about)

3. ????

4. Profit!

"Simple, right?" Sam said, smiling as the other two laughed. "How hard could it be?"

"The problem," Allen said, "is that we're still all too programmed to think of this whole client-contact relationship like a transaction. We put effort in, we get results back."

"Or like gambling," Becca added. "Play enough times, one of your bets has to hit." They nodded in agreement.

"My senior partner calls it dialing for dollars," Sam said. "I'm thinking that was some old game show or something. Before my time. But you get the idea, right? Blunt-force attacks."

"On a basic level, it makes sense," Becca said. "You make enough bets, you drop enough lines in the water—is that right? I don't fish—you're bound to get something to go your way sooner or later."

"Yes, but trust me, sometimes something is worse than nothing," Allen said. "I can't tell you how much time I've spent chasing down lead after lead, using up hour after hour, only to end up with a meager little client engagement. There's so much more that could be done so much more effectively, and at my company we're certainly not doing it."

"Not doing what?" Candace said, leaning into the conference room. "I could see you folks going on and on about something in here," she said, pointing at the windows. "Pretty much the whole shop could."

"You like our new formula for contacts?" Sam said, pointing at the whiteboard. "We're pretty proud of it."

Candace laughed. "Number three is especially perceptive," she said. "I'm so proud of you guys."

"Thank you," Sam said, "but look, we have no idea what you're looking for here. We know what we've done in the past. We know it hasn't worked out so well for any of us. Beyond that? We don't know very much."

"Cut yourself some slack, Sam," Candace said. "The good thing is, this is like riding a bike. You already know how to start pedaling. I'm going to teach you how to go down steep hills and weave through traffic."

"Helmets on?" Becca smiled.

"Helmets on," Candace said, wiping the whiteboard clean and writing "CONTEXT" in the blank space. "The word *context* doesn't really have a precise definition, and that's appropriate because it's a word that you apply differently depending on different situations. You need to understand the changing environment and, as best you can, determine what your contact is seeking. There's no one-size-fits-all approach."

"Example, please," Allen said.

"In football you can draw up a play right down to the individual steps," Candace said. "It's one of the things I love about the game. You can see the timing, the precision, the way that the quarterback and the receiver connect right down to the second." She started to draw something on the whiteboard, then thought better of it.

"I'm not a football coach. I wouldn't even know where to begin." She smiled.

"You need a whistle," Becca said.

"That would help. Anyway, it's interesting to see a football team carry out a precise play. But what's even more interesting is to see how the team responds when everything all of a sudden falls apart. When the defense has picked up what you're doing and is actively trying to stop you. How do you compensate? What do you do to make sure the defense doesn't get what it wants, which is, make no mistake, to stop you in your tracks?"

They said nothing.

"I can tell you what won't work," Candace continued. "Doing the same thing you've done before, doing the same thing everyone else has done before you. The defense studies film, too. They can smell your weak games a mile away."

"Wait, I'm a little confused," Sam said. "Who exactly is the defense in this scenario?"

"Anybody or anything who keeps you from making that connection with the right prospective client," Candace said. "You may think of it as the client himself, putting up a defense against the same-old, same-old sales pitches. Or you may think it is the client's administrative staff, making sure you don't get a fair shake or any face time. I prefer, though, that you think of the client as your teammate, not your opposition. Put yourself on the same side of the playing field with them and the defense becomes anybody or anything that keeps you from helping that prospect solve their big challenges—the ones you are so great at solving. Then you're like the offensive line—operating in a way that helps the quarterback execute without getting sacked. Then it's you and the client against an external defense blocking the goal line. That obstacle could be external circumstances from market conditions to organizational politics or from bad weather to missed connections to technology problems. Whatever it is, you've got to be sure that you can get past that defense by helping the client advance with you. And," she added, pointing for emphasis, "you'll note that each one of those defenses requires a different style of playmaking."

"Makes sense," Sam said. "But look, that's a lot of decision making on the fly, isn't it?"

"A quarterback has to make a dozen decisions in about three seconds, and so does each offensive lineman," Candace said. "If you train your brain to recognize and react, you're going to be that much better at seeing potential problems even before they arise." She pulled out a chair and sat down.

"Consider, Sam, that first day you came in here. You were all depressed and down about that prospect meeting going so badly. You remember?"

"I've been trying to kill the memory of that for a while now." Sam smiled. "Thanks for bringing it back."

"No problem. That was the defense I had to get past, your preoccupation. Pretty much the last thing you were interested in was anything I had to offer beyond a bit of shelter. You could have gotten that at any fast-food joint within five miles. I had to get past your biases and your defenses and show you that we have more to offer here at The Open Note."

"So how did you do it?" Becca asked. "Obviously it worked."

"I think Sam could tell you," Candace said.

"It was the cookies." Sam smiled, and the others nodded in understanding.

"Of course it was the cookies," Candace said. "Cookies, especially warm ones, touch on something primal, something from childhood. Even if you know you're not supposed to have them, you can usually talk yourself into at least one. And then I've got you."

"You make it sound like Sam's a fish you just reeled in," Allen said.

"Yes and no," Candace said. "You've got to prove that you've got more to offer than the next shop down the line. And that means one cookie's not enough. You've got to deliver more than that."

She stood up and motioned around the entire coworking area. "Look, if we were just a coffee shop, would we be able to sustain ourselves? Probably not. We'd get crushed under the boot heels of the big guys. But we combine coffee with a sense of home and togetherness and a sense of possibility and opportunity for your business."

"And it all starts with a cookie."

"And it all starts with a cookie," she agreed. "The cookie gives me a good insight into whether you're the kind of person who might benefit from our particular brand of hospitality. The cookie shows who we are right up front. And granted, some people don't want cookies. They want their coffee and they want to be gone. There's nothing wrong with that. But for those who want more, well . . ." She made a small motion to encompass the table. "We hope they'll find it rewarding."

"How do you decide who gets a cookie?" Becca asked.

"Well, everyone gets a cookie to start, or at least the opportunity to get one," Candace replied. "I train the staff to be on the lookout for a very specific type: someone who's not just here for a transaction, someone who might be suited for a longer-term connection."

"You also look for the sad sacks," Sam said.

"I wouldn't put it exactly that way, but yes, we do consider the emotional component," Candace said. "It's not just about appealing to the head, you know. Going for the heart lets you bypass some of the resistance that the head is likely to mount. Keep that in mind."

The three were furiously scribbling "HEART > HEAD" or some equivalent as Candace turned to go. She stopped and nodded to herself.

"Put your pencils down," she said. "No, wait; pick them up again. Just stop writing what you were writing. Write this instead." She paused, forming the thoughts in her head. "I've got a homework assignment for you. I want each of you to get out in the world and do some actual heavy lifting."

"Literal heavy lifting?" Sam said. "You want us to unload your trucks, don't you?"

"No, no, no, smart guy," she replied. "I'm assuming you've all made at least some new connections in the last few weeks." They nodded. "Excellent. You've opened the door; now it's time to charge through." She lifted a hand to cut off Sam's already-forming comment. "Not literally charge through. I don't need you getting thrown out of any more offices, Sam."

They all laughed at that, even Sam, who had come to frame his disastrous interview as a source of strength rather than shame.

"So here's what I want you to do," Candace continued. "Pick a contact and set up that 'next meeting.' And before you have that next meeting, prepare yourself. Don't just show up expecting to dazzle them with your perfect teeth. No, I want you to do two things—and this is where you can write again."

They obediently began taking notes. "First," Candace continued, "figure out a reason for having this conversation, and no, 'I want you as a client' is not a good enough reason. Find a good enough reason for them. What's happening in their lives, in their business, in their world that you can help illuminate and clarify? Connect with content."

"Sounds good," Allen said. "What's the second thing?"

"Give them a cookie," Candace said. "Not literally, unless you want to. But that might be a bit strange. No, what I want you to do is give them a sense of what it would be like to work with you, to have you in their professional cadre. But it's got to be in a way that benefits them, not you. Show them you're original. Show them you're the kind of person someone wants to work with. Show them that you can deliver value and quality and that you're someone worth knowing right this very minute. Not just because of what you do but because of how you do it and because of who you are. Let them feel it. Let them experience it. Before they hire you. Give them a taste . . . a sample."

She paused, looking around at them. "You're already thinking of how you can do this, aren't you?" she said.

"Absolutely," Becca said. "It starts to take on a new shape when you break out of the usual routine."

Candace nodded. "That's exactly right. I know you guys like football, right?" All three agreed that they did. "Me too. Would put it on here in the café if I didn't think it would alter the entire atmosphere. If you ever watch the quarterback, you know that he never throws it where a receiver is; he throws it where a receiver's going to be, often before the hole's even visible. It's amazing. You anticipate, you expect, you project—and then you're ready when it's your moment." She paused for a moment.

"It's your moment," Candace said. "Get out there and claim it. Go win one for the Gipper."

SET THE TONE FOR THE TEAM

21

Coach's Commentary

It's a truism in sports that teams model themselves on the persona and mindset of the head coach. Passionate coaches can inspire their teams to ever-greater heights; callow or indecisive coaches quickly lose their locker rooms. Your clients become part of your team, and it's up to you to keep them engaged, motivated, and working together with you. If they start to drift, it might not be their fault; it might be yours.

> If fitting the right business development tactics to the right situation is the "what" of context, setting the right tone and truthfulness refer to the "how" of it.

Since the publication of Joe Pine and Jim Gilmore's seminal book *The Experience Economy* more than a decade ago, business and professional services firms have been much more attuned to crafting engaging client experiences, specifically in the way they treat organizations and their executives *after* they've become paying clients. The next step in this evolution is for firms to become far more intentional about transforming their prospect experiences.

The question is, How do you orchestrate each touch point along the path of the prospect's encounter with you and your firm even *before* the prospect becomes a paying client?

Did you notice how in the game film Candace laid this groundwork masterfully? From the way she greets new visitors to the café to the way she opens the coworking space to a handpicked group of outsiders for highly exclusive thought leadership and networking events, she's thought this through. Like the director of a Broadway play, Candace has carefully considered how she wants her audience to respond to her theater of coffee and connections. How do you want your prospective clients to think and feel as you open and advance the relationship with them?

The goal is to increase your likability and trustworthiness in each step of the experience and in each conversation along the way. *Tone* and *truth* are the means to achieve this goal. Tone defines how you secure and engage those conversations. Truth is a matter of delivering each prospect experience with authenticity and continuity with your existing message.

To get smarter about the tone you set, train your eyes and ears by listening to others and watching them in action.

Practice identifying genuine versus contrived speech. Notice whether you are more likely to pay attention to a friendly voice or to one that is dull and monotonous or frustrated and angry. (I think you can successfully predict the outcome of that experiment.) Speak like a human talking with another human, not a sales robot or a game show host. Energy and enthusiasm are attention-grabbing and contagious, but only if they're for real. See if you can find something to be enthusiastic about in every encounter you have.

We get bought for our affability as much as for our capability, not just what we do but how we do it. If you approach contacts with the proper context, you can use your affability to affirm your capability. If you avoid displaying desperation, no matter how desperate you may feel, you'll see the payoff.

One of the clichés in sales is "It's not what you say, it's how you say it." This has been so overused that people have forgotten how true it really is. The same words with a different tone lead to different results. Let us say this with all the genuine passion and enthusiasm we can muster: *approaching your prospects in a relaxed, upbeat, and confident way is at least as important as what you are actually saying.* Cheerful, comforting, and convincing is the alliteration to remember.

Other elements that set the tone for a positive prospect experience include what your prospects see when they come to your website or LinkedIn page and how they see you out in the community. They're looking at you and asking themselves, Does this person and his or her firm understand people like me and companies like mine? Who do they spend time with? Whom do they serve? Are those the people and companies that we aspire to be like?

You know what guilt by association is. Honor by association is its inverse.

The people and organizations with which you associate and the places where you work and play influence a prospect's perception of your reputation and capability. That's not to say you should fake any of these things or participate in them despite your distaste for certain people, places, and ways. Instead, you must be mindful about their alignment with your opening strategy.

Congruence is a key factor in crafting the right context. Suppose you hold a new prospect encounter in a conference room at the Ritz-Carlton Hotel. The meeting table is shiny walnut with a porcelain tea setting and an orchid centerpiece. Throughout the meeting you are clear, concise, relevant, and appropriately attentive. When it comes time to provide a leave-behind about your firm, you pull the documents out of a plastic grocery bag, flick some food particles from the cover, and toss the tattered, coffee-stained brochure to your prospect. That's incongruence—when something you do or say is inconsistent with your stated or standard behavior.

Incongruence is the inconsistency that dissolves trust.

What do you think of your odds of winning the business when incongruence like that exists?

During the prospect experience, future clients of choice will prefer your candor to your hesitancy. They will prefer your emotional generosity to your smoke screen. One way to demonstrate this is to use your early conversations to unveil the full reality of their circumstances so that you can help them more completely deal with the real issues they face. The idea here is to assure them that you're sharing in their problems, that you're exploring solutions together.

You want the tone to be "same team, same side of the table." With that approach, with that tone, you'll establish an atmosphere of mutual trust and respect that will keep your clients at your side, not at your throat.

PLAY THE ODDS

22

Roll Game Film

The cursor on Sam's computer screen blinked continuously, the way it had for the last 90 minutes. Sam didn't have time to check e-mail, Facebook, or LinkedIn or to waste time on any other distractions. As he sat in his office this morning, he had a long list of potential calls that he'd be working through before he even thought about digging for new ones. The art of the contact, a moment he'd once dreaded, had become, thanks to Candace, an opportunity for opening new doors.

"Sam?" It was Roger Smith's voice on Sam's phone. "Sam? Come in here."

Opening new doors . . . and closing a few old ones.

Sam was aware that Roger had been checking out his client expense statements and knew that he was keeping a close eye on how much time Sam was spending on each contact. Sam had known this day was coming eventually.

"What can I do for you, Roger?" he said, walking into the senior partner's office and taking a seat. He noticed for the first time that Roger's decor matched his persona: loud yet exceedingly conventional. The artwork consisted of replicas, and the furniture was the kind of off-the-shelf style you'd see in a model home. There was nothing memorable here, Sam thought, nothing to encourage you to return.

"Sam," Roger said, bringing Sam out of his reverie, "I've got to say that I'm not exactly pleased with how your client development efforts are coming along. You're talking to the same people over and over again. You're not hitting new clients often enough."

"Sir," Sam replied, "this is a new approach I'm taking. The idea is not to stack up a bunch of one-off clients but to build relationships for the long term. That takes more than a quick phone call and a handshake."

"It's time, Sam, and time is something we don't have in tremendous supply in this firm," Roger said. "I want you out there hitting the streets, finding what you can when you can, picking up clients as often as you can. You know what I'm going to say here . . ."

"I do," Sam replied. "Dialing for dollars."

"Dialing for dollars," Roger agreed. "The more you dial, the more you make. It's science."

But science, or whatever Roger thought passed for it, was exactly what wasn't needed in this situation, Sam thought. It was much more art than science. He'd secured three clients since his pair of disastrous client visits, and all of those clients seemed interested in the long haul with him. Granted, it had required nurturing and finesse, but when he'd reached those deals, he'd felt almost as good as when he'd secured his employment.

Sam stood up and thanked Roger for his advice, assuring him that he'd increase the number of calls and bring home some more clients for the firm. Roger shook his hand, engaging in some of the painfully awkward small talk that Sam could now see for what it was. Yes, the weather's great; no, I didn't see the game last night; sure, some golf sometime soon would be a lot of fun.

The words of old grip-and-grin hucksters like Roger still had some merit, certainly. But as Sam had recognized in the last few weeks, the changing business environment meant that new conversational and opening techniques were necessary, techniques that Roger simply couldn't or wouldn't grasp. His proclamations no longer carried the weight of gospel.

Sam looked over his to-contact list. Certainly, Roger's ideas of keeping a steady stream of contacts in the pipeline had merit. You don't want to be too dependent on any one client, and you don't want to be too desperate for any one contact to turn into a client. That was sound, reasonable advice no matter who it came from.

But the transactional approach—networking to close a single deal—now seemed absurdly limited to Sam. Chasing the dollars for one engagement was a limited-use proposition. Also, Sam had never shaken the sense that Roger's dialing for dollars approach was a form of cell-phone stalking.

What it all added up to was a change in perspective, a change in the way Sam approached every single relationship in his life—yes, even the one with Roger. He now understood the way to keep everything in its proper perspective in order to keep everything moving forward. It was all beginning to pay off, little by little.

His phone chirped, and Sam saw that Becca was texting him. "Lunch? My treat."

"Three of my favorite words," Sam texted back. They made plans to meet at a new tapas bar midway between their offices in a couple of hours, and Sam dived back into his work.

When he arrived for lunch, he was feeling flush. The morning had gone well; he'd set up half a dozen get-togethers and felt he was close to getting to the next level, so to speak, with several other contacts. He could feel the tide turning in his favor.

And as soon as he saw Becca, he could see that it wasn't turning in hers. She looked flustered, frustrated, fidgety. Once they'd ordered, he got her to open up about why.

"It's just not clicking for me," Becca said. "I see you and Allen doing so well with what Candace has shown us, and I just can't seem to crack the code. I'm no better now than when I first started at The Open Note."

"Well, you're aware there's a problem, and sometimes that's the first step that people need to get going," Sam said. "Let's break it down. Where are you trying to make contacts?"

"Where am I not?" Becca said. "I'm telling everyone I know to tell everyone they know about what I've got to offer. I've put ads in church bulletins, I've tacked up notices in every coffee shop around town. I've bought ad space on Facebook—"

"Wait," Sam said. "You're advertising your professional services with ads in coffee shops?"

"Yes," Becca said. "I figure the more people who see the ad, the more likely it is that someone's going to reach out to me. Is that wrong?"

"Well, not wrong per se but maybe not the most right thing you could be doing," Sam said. "Remember what Candace said about context. You've got to reach people at the right time in the right way. Even if the right person somehow manages to be in the coffee shop and spot one of your ads, are people really in a mood to hire you for your services while they're in line for a latte?"

Becca nodded. "Good point."

"There's a little bit tougher one to consider," Sam said. "What does it say about you as a professional if someone's seeing your work right next to an ad for free kittens? That's not the kind of image you want to be putting forth."

"I never really thought of it that way."

"Neither did I until very recently. But Candace has taught me that we've got to consider not just our message itself but the environment around our message. There's so much more to it than just throwing out what we want wherever we can get it out there."

Becca had begun taking notes again, precise ones that looked like they'd come from a printer. "It goes against everything we were taught, doesn't it?"

"It does, but it's important sometimes to leave behind the past," Sam said. "You've got to think of yourself not as a beggar but as a *resource*. You've got something to offer, and people ought to be aware of it."

"Thank you!" The gratitude and relief were evident on Becca's face.

"Of course. Matter of fact, I'm going to need your help on something I've got going on," Sam said. "Let's make a plan to get together on that soon."

Becca took out her planner. She meticulously counted forward four business days and wrote "CALL SAM" on it. Then she wrote a list of questions she'd ask him.

"Sorry to pry," Sam said, "but what exactly are you doing there?"

"Setting up plans to contact you again," Becca said. "I always wait exactly four days to contact someone. That way, I've given them time to figure out where they are and what I can do for them before I check in with them."

Sam winced. "You know that checking in is about the worst thing you can do."

Becca looked genuinely confused. "Why? Isn't that what we're supposed to be doing?"

"Checking in for the sake of checking in adds nothing except frustration to your contact," Sam said. "You've got to find something more subtle, some way that you can deliver value to them even when you're just saying hello. Here's one thing I like to do: fire over a couple of links to articles that they may not have seen but are relevant to them. Point out to them what it is you think they should especially look at in the articles and indicate what you think might be the implications for them. That way they know you're not just spamming the same thing out to everyone. You've actually thought about them specifically. It's not foolproof, but sometimes it can get a conversation started where there wasn't one before."

"You don't mind if I write that down, do you?"

"Touché." Sam smiled. He pulled out a few sugar packets and laid them on the table. "When I used to play quarterback, I had a huge problem. When the defense was coming at me—" He moved the packets around. "—I panicked. I didn't know what to do when things weren't as they'd been drawn up, so I tended to just throw the ball away."

"And how did that turn out?"

"Not well." Sam laughed. "If I was lucky, the ball fell to the ground incomplete. If I wasn't so lucky, I'd get nailed for intentional grounding. And if I was really, really unlucky, the defense would intercept it. I was really unlucky a lot." They laughed together. "The point is, I couldn't get on the right page with my receivers and I couldn't account for the defense, so I'd just do what was best for me. It rarely worked out properly. That's what seems to happen when I just call to check in."

Becca nodded. "I get what you're saying."

They finished the meal with some conversation about nothing in particular and went their separate ways with a smile. Sam was feeling strong about his future prospects, but he knew he needed to stop by The Open Note. He had a purchase to make.

"Sam!" Candace said. "What brings you here? You're not usually in today."

Sam told her about the meeting with Becca, about the way he understood the role of authenticity rather than artifice. "And that reminded me of something," he said, motioning toward the sailboat painting that was still hanging on the wall. The previous weekend, Sam finally had gotten around to visiting Captain Barnard and his art boat at Heaven Harbor. Candace had been right. He was the real deal. Clearly Barnard had suffered terribly from the toll of war, but he had emerged triumphant in his own way. He had found his art and an unstoppable creative vision that was his salvation.

With one hand, Sam reached for his wallet. With the other, he touched the handmade frame of Captain Barnard's boat.

"I'll be hanging that on my wall now."

GET MORE FIRST DOWNS

23

Coach's Commentary

Timing is an essential component of context, and it has three dimensions that are most relevant for opening relationships and revenue: accuracy, frequency, and longevity. To say that business development success is a numbers game is a bit misleading. Yes, it is important to reach enough of the right people, and if you reach them in the wrong way at the wrong time, the door slams in your face and stays closed. Business development is less like a numbers game and more like a numbers tightrope walk.

ACCURACY

If having the right number of prospect and referral source conversations at the right time is a tightrope walk, your balancing pole is an awareness of timing that's in your prospect's best interest rather than your own. In sports such as baseball and cricket, powerful batting is a matter of timing rather than strength. Timing means your swing meets the ball at the right impact point, at just the right moment. Great timing comes with reading the pitcher's or bowler's release, seeing the ball earlier as it approaches you, and knowing what to look for in its flight path.

> Great timing in business development means reading your prospect's business objectives, watching for trigger points that affect the prospect's goal achievement, and helping the prospect know how to respond.

The more attuned your early warning system is—the more you've equipped referral sources and arranged for a stream of insights about your prospects to flow exclusively in your direction—the more accurate you will be in your timing.

FREQUENCY

How many contacts and how many touches are enough? It depends. If you have value to bring, more is better. If you have none, one is too many. Getting in front of *more* of the right prospects is important. Quantity matters.

> During my 18 years I came to bat almost 10,000 times. I struck out about 1,700 times and walked maybe 1,800 times. You figure a ballplayer will average about 500 at bats a season. That means I played seven years without ever hitting the ball.
>
> —Mickey Mantle
>
> I've missed more than 9,000 shots in my career. I've lost almost 300 games. Twenty-six times, I've been trusted to take the game winning shot and missed. I've failed over and over and over again in my life. And that is why I succeed.
>
> —Michael Jordan

Do you get 10,000 at bats in business development? Do you get 9,000 shots? Unlikely.

How many do you get? How many more is enough? How many prospects do you need to generate a new client?

How many more of the right touches does it take with any single prospect to convert a prospect into a new client? As many as it takes.

How many *wrong* phone calls does it take to close a prospect's door forever? One.

In football, intentional grounding is an incomplete pass thrown by a quarterback toward an area of the field where there is clearly no eligible receiver, usually in a desperate attempt to avoid getting sacked. It makes the quarterback look bad and results in a penalty: 10 yards and loss of a down. In business development, the equivalent is making calls just to check in. Quit doing that. It makes you look like a peddler trolling for sales and results in a decrease in trust. In your case, perhaps it has been unintentional, but it is relationship grounding nonetheless. In fact, any disingenuous behavior transparently done for your own benefit will dilute relationship rapport. That's not how you want to play. That's the wrong timing.

It shouldn't surprise anyone that the quarterback with the largest number of pass attempts in his career—Brett Favre with 10,169—is also the one with the most pass completions (6,300). Throw the ball when you have an eligible receiver in the open field. Get up to bat as often as possible. Find and pursue as many opportunities to offer your services as possible.

Follow the right order of operations and repeat that sequence continuously. That's quantity.

Look for the right pitch. Swing the good swing. Spend your time with the right prospects. Each time you reach out to a prospect, have a relationship advancement goal in mind and substantive content in hand.

Connect with content of value again and again. That's quality.

LONGEVITY

Longevity means being a ready resource for your prospects over time: the more you're in the game, the more you're likely to get a hit. Baseball legend Pete Rose holds the record for the most career hits (4,256) in part because he also played the most career games (3,562) and had the most at bats (14,053) of anyone who ever played the game.

In advisory professions and complex business services, it is sometimes unclear when the right prospect need will arise, and so you need to stay in front of your most vital connections consistently over the very long haul. The key question is how you maintain a high degree of diligence and endurance so that you can keep going. Like a great athlete, you need to stay in shape and be ready to pivot to stay in the game over time. Keep yourself up to date, agile, and fast. All this is true but is not enough. Diligence and endurance come not just from skill and competitiveness but from a pure love of what you do. If the process of opening and sustaining business relationships feels like drudgery, reexamine your personal mission (your "why") and reprioritize your prospects. Spend more time with prospects who feel like they could be true friends as well as clients. Find the raison d'être that impels you constantly forward.

Need inspiration? Look to any of the great athletes who continued to play far beyond the average player age in their sport. George Blanda, the longtime Oakland Raiders quarterback and kicker, played more seasons in the NFL—26—than any other player to date. His colleagues claim that it was the fire in his belly and love of competition that kept him in top form all those years. Blanda retired just before his forty-ninth birthday.

At age 64, swimmer Diana Nyad was the first person to complete the 103-mile swim from Cuba to Florida without stopping and without the protection of a shark cage. She prevailed on her fifth attempt after failing previously as a result of a range of physically brutal conditions, from swarms of sharks and jellyfish stings to asthma attacks, severe storms, and sheer exhaustion. Nyad had dreamed of completing the historic swim since she was eight years old. That's how a personal mission fuels endurance and permits a champion to stay in the game until victory.

The accompanying figure provides a summary of the elements of the key context factors that will hasten your pace across the open field.

04   *Right Context*

- **TONE**
  - Cheerful
  - Comforting
  - Convincing

- **TRUTH**
  - Authenticity
  - Congruence

- **TIMING**
  - Accuracy
  - Frequency
  - Longevity

SECTION 6
OPEN-ENDED

STAY OPEN

24

Roll Game Film

SIX MONTHS LATER

Candace pushed through the hanging plastic at what had once been the far edge of The Open Note's coworking space and embraced Sam, Allen, and Becca in turn. She laughed as she saw that she'd gotten construction dust on all three of them.

"What do you think?" Candace said. "We've expanded into next door here. We've got three other branches opening up next quarter in our biggest markets yet. It's all coming together!"

"Looks great, Candace," Sam said. "You should be so proud."

"I am!" she gushed. "I'd offer each of you a cookie, but I'm afraid they'd be covered in sawdust."

"When's the grand reopening?" Becca asked. "I'm trying to schedule a seminar, and I'd love to have it here."

"And we'd love to have you," Candace replied. "Two weeks from now we'll be up and running." She turned to Allen. "And you, sir. I owe you a huge thanks!"

"You're welcome, of course," Allen said. "But why?"

"You, Mr. Golden Contact List, have sent me some of the biggest names in the city. You thought I wouldn't pick up on the fact that the mayor, the governor, and three different football players have come through here on your recommendation?"

"Just doing what I can." Allen smiled. "You taught us to always have something to offer. I've got quite the asset to offer right here."

Candace nodded in gratitude. "You've done some tremendous good for me. Did you see the write-up on us last week in the paper? Well, on the paper's website. It's brought in so many new customers!"

"None as good as the earlier ones, though, right?" Sam smiled.

"Let's just say we're still in the earliest phase of the customer relationship process with many of them," Candace said. "But you know, that's why I asked you three to come here even though we're under construction."

"Glad you let us in," Allen said. "We were going to have to hold our weekly gathering over at—"

"Don't even say it," Candace said. "You three will have special reserved chairs here. Part of The Open Note's new executive-level privileges. And in those chairs, I'll want you to go over this for me." She reached into a briefcase and handed each one of them a folder.

"It's a prospectus for our national rollout," she said. "I'd like your professional input. And you—" She turned to Sam. "—I'd like your professional services."

"Me? But you know this is out of my league."

"Right. You should know by now, Sam, I'm about building relationships, not just business transactions. Sure, there's somebody out there with more experience. But I know you've got the right philosophy and the right approach to look out for me."

"Plus he's a lot cheaper," Becca added.

"Plus you're a lot cheaper." Candace laughed. "Of course, if this works out, there'll be room for all of you at the table. And I'm hoping we'll have more to offer you than just chocolate chip cookies."

Sam looked over the prospectus, liking what he saw and liking even more what he heard. "I'm in," he said, shaking Candace's hand.

"Perfect," she said, escorting them to a table. "Now, how about we all sit down and talk about what's coming next?"

WINNING IN THE RED ZONE

25

Coach's Commentary

It's common sense though not common practice: a quarterback who executes enough of the right plays successfully finds that he regularly leads his team into the red zone—the area inside the opponent's 20-yard line, where the odds of scoring rise significantly. Professionals who open enough contextually appropriate conversations with enough of the right prospects and referral sources often enough will more frequently find that prospective clients open the door to the red zone for them. Quite often, you'll be invited into the end zone because you've earned that right. However, you can't count on it.

All your opening work can be fumbled in the red zone if you don't recognize when you're there and play accordingly. In football, playing in the red zone means playing with a compressed field against a steadfast defense that tightens the space further. With the need for quicker quarterback releases and limited passing and running options as more of the defense crowds the line of scrimmage the closer the offense gets to the goal line, teams develop whole playbooks focused on winning in the red zone. Offensive coordinators pick red zone plays such as pin plays and scissors plays, fade routes and sweep plays, and back-shoulder throws. But it is the mental game that matters most in this space. Players who can stay cool, relaxed, and in the moment without overthinking can win the day. Those who overcomplicate things and try too hard tend to choke. The same is true in business development.

You know you're choking in the business development red zone
when you find yourself shifting from genuine to manipulative and
from cooperative to competitive.

When you see the prospect as your competitor rather than the challenge the prospect faces as your collective competition, you are at risk of breaking the trust that brought you to the opportunity in the first place.

If your prospects don't automatically hand you a signed work order without your asking, here are some words you can use to advance from prospect/advisor to client/advisor status:

Reinforce your capability. Verify that they believe you're the answer.

- "Based on our discussion so far, it seems like we're well suited to support you on this project. Do you see it the same way?"

Reinforce your affability and affinity. Show your enthusiasm for working with them and your confidence in a great result.

- "We would love to work with you and your team."

Package it for them. Very specifically spell out the activities you will perform, the time frame for execution, and the targeted results. Give them a foolproof plan they can sell in their organization.

- "Here's how it would work."

Let them drive. You've been respectful and collaborative as you've cultivated and opened this relationship. Don't turn Attila the Hun just because you finally smell money.

- "May we move forward on this? How do you suggest we proceed?"

- "What may we do to help you get support to move forward? Here's what's worked in other situations."

- "Would you consider including us in the RFP process?"

Start the ball rolling. Make a presumptive move forward on the engagement.

- "We will begin collecting the data we need to help right away."

- "We'll start to schedule our key process-checkpoint meetings now."

- "What do you need from us to get started?"

Finally, remind new clients how glad you are to be working with them on their critical matters. Keep in mind Humphrey Bogart's famous line at the end of the classic film *Casablanca*: "I think this is the beginning of a beautiful friendship." And keep opening the relationship.

CODA AND
RESOURCES

26

He circled the conference table like the bizarre hybrid offspring of a Bengal tiger and Gordon Gekko, hair slicked back, eyes wild, nostrils flared. "If you can't convert at least one of your clients to a $1.2 million contract—full-page four-color ad in every issue of our magazine—twelve times a year, I'll find other salespeople who can," he bellowed as he slammed his fist on the mahogany table. Papers and pens leaped an inch from the surface, as did butts from seats. A chill went through the room.

In the days when analog media still mattered, the death eater at our throats published a nationally acclaimed magazine in which one page of advertising in one issue cost a marketer $100,000. Persuading companies to spend that much money each month just for our singular publication in some cases meant capturing their *entire* ad budget. Thus, trying to convince them that our one publication would suffice to solely carry their company's message to potential buyers was ballsy, to say the least.

"You are all replaceable," the inflamed publisher continued, "You need to sell *like your lives depend on it*. Because, at least, your *livelihoods* will."

I was twenty-three years old when I sat in that Manhattan conference room, quivering at the command. That night, I returned home to carry out my orders, and I knew whom I needed to contact in the morning: the only company, in fact, that I thought could stomach spending $1.2 million to advertise in one publication. At the time, the business I had in mind spent nearly $250,000—not a paltry sum then or now—with our company each year and was my largest client. Now I would ask them to spend everything they had with me.

The client looked as though he had been a University of Georgia linebacker in his youth. He still carried the hulking frame and humorless scowl. Our visit lasted just 15 minutes, and in that time I sold as if my life depended on it. I persuaded, pushed, asserted, cajoled, and pleaded; I tried every tip, trick, and technique the sales gurus had concocted; and, of course, I closed, closed, closed. I seem to remember my client trying to get a word in edgewise—which I believe was the word *no*—but to no avail, until he hauled his hefty mass of flesh from his leather chair and nearly vaulted his desk with the agility of a blitzing defender. "Get up," he commanded, and physically escorted me out of the building. Never to return again. No $1.2 million. No more $250,000.

Almost 30 years of business experience later, I have stumbled and recovered and succeeded through myriad client interactions as a marketing consultant, a business development coach, and a strategic growth advisor to major business and professional services firms.

> The difference in approach remains clear: the efficacy and return on investment of an opening invitation far outweigh the transgressions of a closing attack.

Create the circumstances for your client to step toward you (I repeat, *step*, not leap angrily) rather than thrusting yourself into the client's space.

For most professionals, business development requires a gymnast's balance between driving forward with urgency and gliding easily with relaxed confidence. You want every worthwhile new client you can attract, and you don't need any. Somewhere between all or nothing and no big deal, you feel your way across the high wire.

Of course, volume matters. The more viable referrals and on-target prospects you have, the more likely it is that a profitable client engagement will emerge at any particular time. Everyone you connect with in some way may be of help to you professionally. You just never know who knows whom and how an encounter may boomerang to benefit or bite you. Therefore, each conversation you have is important, and each one carries high potential.

At the same time, when we approach any single connection with the sense that our jobs depend on successfully closing an engagement with that person, we are apt to behave in a way that destroys trust. In that mindset, anxiety becomes visible, our senses dim, and our discussions shift for the worse. You position yourself opposite prospective clients, coercing them to buy something they don't want rather than standing on the same side of the field with them, working together to solve their business issues.

Instead, imagine (whether or not it is true) that it really doesn't matter if this one project comes through or that a specific connection pays off. You've got plenty to keep you going. If it isn't this one, it will be the next. It's okay. You want to help them. You are best equipped to help them if they want to be helped. But for you, it is not mission-critical. No big deal. If in fact any one potential engagement is going to make or break you or your firm, it's time to find another firm or another profession. Opening means entering each encounter with the underlying sense that *this one discussion isn't so desperately essential*. You can take the time to open the relationship and keep it open. This means focusing attention not on the winning or losing of the sale but on being a great client advisor and collaboratively moving the ball down the field.

If you're still not convinced about opening, open your mind to this: the next generation of professionals is outnumbering the rest, and they're not much into the hard sell. Our characters Sam, Alex, and Becca all fit into this category.

Perhaps because they've grown up in the most overmarketed, media-intensive era ever, today's rising professionals have an inherent distrust of sales. They don't want to sell, and they don't want to be sold.

This worker cohort is accustomed to everyone-is-a-winner collaborative team play, but they're busy banging heads inside firms where business development remains a zero-sum solo sport and where competition eats collaboration for breakfast.

Outside the firm, cultural forces pull the rising generation in a radically more collaborative direction. They share their lives in collaborative conversation with the world through social networks. They eschew ownership for sharing—who needs to buy a Prius when you can borrow the Zipcar when you need it? Collaborative, casual coworking spaces such as Candace's Open Note are for real and are on the rise. Still, if millennials can't find a way to grow their firms' revenue and relationships, their careers will stall and their firms will fail. Senior professionals must address this succession challenge now or they'll be inadvertently designing their regression plan. Opening is the antidote.

When you stay open, a multitude of benefits come your way:

Profit. When it is consistently applied, opening allows you to attract your clients of choice: those whose lifetime value to you far outstrips the benefit of short-term clients coerced with closing tactics. Opening encourages a collaborative business development approach that increases your odds of winning larger-scale client work and has the benefit of making your firm more attractive to the best young professional talent. In this case, the firm you have built will pay dividends beyond today.

Professional. Opening behavior is authentic and credible, and as a result, applying Opening Playbook concepts helps enhance your professional reputation.

Personal. When you put yourself in a position to be bought—inviting the client to step forward to engage you—your mind is taken off the urgent need to close the deal. In this more natural relationship-building mode, professionals find themselves working with clients and prospects who feel like friends rather than combatants. They actually begin to enjoy business development.

Physical. Then there is the substantial physical health benefit that comes with opening. Okay, opening isn't going to lower your cholesterol or anything, but you will be much less likely to be bodily tossed out of an office. So there's that.

Open-mindedness is a two-way communication skill. Close-mindedness is one-way. Bluster, puffery, arrogance, and linear thinking are the closing weapons of charlatans. Humility, empathy, conviction, and lateral thinking are the opening gifts of great advisors.

Open. Stay open. Keep on opening.

OPENING RESOURCES

Here are some tools to help you cruise along the opening path:

Playbook on a page. The infographic shown on the next page gives you the top-line elements of the Opening Playbook—you can download a version of it online at www.openingplaybook.com. Print it out, put it on your wall or in your pocket, and refer to it regularly.

Coaching business developers. When you not only have to bring in the work yourself but also have to coach others to do it, you may welcome a few extra ideas on how to stay sane and successful. I've put together a Coach the Coaches primer for you that is available for downloading at www.openingplaybook.com.

Growing professional services. This is my ongoing blog, where you'll find new ideas and inspiration to help you build a thriving practice. I welcome your participation. Visit www.growingprofessionalservices.com.

Client Advisor Awards. This annual awards program recognizes world-class professional services firms that deliver extraordinary client experiences and results. As you can imagine, firms and professionals that engage prospective and existing clients in the opening process score higher than do those that don't. The Client Advisor Awards program also recognizes clients of choice: those whose opening behavior enables professional advisors to deliver the best possible outcomes for their client organizations. Are you a world-class client or professional advisor? Find out at www.clientadvisorawards.com.

Creative Growth Group. This is where you can find my colleagues and me. Stop by. Say hello. Let's find a way to help each other. The virtual door is always open at www.creativegrowthgroup.com.

01
Right Opening Strategy

1. CLIENTS
2. CAPABILITIES
3. COMPETITORS
4. CONSEQUENCES

02
Right Connections

1. PRIORITIZE
2. CULTIVATE
3. HARVEST

03
Right Conversations

1. CAMPAIGNS
2. CONTENT
3. CURIOSITY
4. COLLABORATION

04
Right Context

1. TONE
2. TRUTH
3. TIMING

INDEX

A

Absolutes, competitors, 68, 74
Accept referrals/introductions, 119–120
The Accidental Creative (Henry), 135
Accuracy, timing opening, 189–190, 193
Activities in capabilities, 65–67
Affiliations, client similarities, 62, 92
Affinity:
    client similarities, 62
    team tone, setting, 180–181
Agility, longevity, 192–193
Any Given Sunday (film), 115
The Art of War (Sun Tzu), xv
Ask for help, referrals/introductions, 117–119
Asking questions (*See* Questions)
Aspirations, client situation, 62
Attributes of competitors, 67–68, 74
Authenticity:
    begin the conversation, 37
    context for conversation, 193
    friendly, 31–32
    as key to success, 26
    opening vs. manipulating, 17–18, 200
    vs. perfection, context of conversation, 168–169
    relationship rhythm, 29–32
    team tone, setting, 179–182
    of your offering, 53–55, 60

The Autobiography of Benjamin Franklin (Franklin), 119
Awards program as delivery platform, 133–134

B

Balance referral sources, 121
Beane, Billy, 16
Ben Franklin effect, 119–120
Blanda, George, 192
Blogs, campaign delivery, 134–135
Blue chip/tier prospects, 87
Bogart, Humphrey, 201
Brett, George, 41
Business development (*See specific topics*)
Buying criteria, client statistics, 61

C

Campaigns vs. tactics, 125
Campaign tiers, 125–137, 209
    experiences, 126–129, 136, 158
    matching to prospects, 136–137
    platforms, 126, 129–134, 136, 158
    programs, 126, 130–137, 158
"Candace" (*See* Roll Game Film)
Capabilities:
    activities, 65–67
    claim to fame, 60, 63–67, 74, 209
    how does it feel?, 63, 65–67, 74

Capabilities (*continued*):
how you do it?, 63–65, 74
Opening Strategy approach, 60, 63–67, 74, 209
reframing, 64
what you do?, 63–64, 74
Casablanca (film), 201
Change as opportunity, 91
Claim to fame, 63–74
authentic offering, 53–55, 60
capabilities, 60, 63–67, 74, 209
competitors, 60, 67–68, 74, 209
Opening Story, 70–71, 73, 117
sequences of plays, 42
testing opening, 71–73
Client Advisor Awards online, 208
Client payoff, consequences, 74
Clients:
acting as advisor toward, 200–201, 205
four S approach, 61–63, 91–93
growth strategies, 88–89
ideal, 61–63, 89–93
know the client, 6, 16, 18
Opening Strategy approach, 60–63, 74, 209
similarities, 61–62, 74, 92
situations, 62–63, 74, 93
statistics, 61, 74, 91
stepping toward you, 204
suitability, 63, 74
(*See also* Prospects; *specific topics*)
Close-mindedness, 207
Closing, opening vs., xi, 16–19
Coach for Coaches online, 208
Coaching and game film (*See* Roll Game Film)
Coach's Commentary (*See* Opening Strategy approach)
Cocreated collaboration, 158
Coin toss, xi–xvi
Collaboration:
acting as client advisor, 200–201, 206
cocreated, 158

in conversations, 144–145, 148, 158, 209
defined, 148
ideas exchanged, 158
productive, 155
Roll Game Film example, 139–146
signals, 155–157
trust, 157
truth seeking, 158
unknown elements, 156–157
Collaborative community, 53–55, 58–59
Comfort in relationship, 30, 181, 193
Communication (*See* Conversations; *specific topics*)
Community as referral sources, 107
Competitors:
absolutes, 68, 74
attributes, 67–68, 74
claim to fame, 60, 67–68, 74, 209
Opening Strategy approach, 60, 67–68, 74, 209
substitutes, 68
Compliance, client situation, 62, 93
Congruence and context, 181–182, 193
Connections:
client growth strategies, 88–89
client similarities, 61–62, 74, 92
consequential, 112
cultivate prospects, 86, 121, 209
harvest prospects, 86, 121, 209
introductions and referrals, 109–120
locker room speech, 109–120
in opening formula, xiv
prioritize prospects, 86–95, 121, 209
receivers, find fast, 109–114
recruiting prospects , 77–95
rhythm establishment, 21–32
sequences of plays, xiv
teamwork for referrals, 97–108
(*See also* Relationships)
Consequences:
client payoff, 74
criteria for success, 69–70

Opening Strategy approach, 60, 69–70, 74, 209
"why?," 74
Content:
connecting with, 152
in conversations, 143, 148–153, 158, 209
defined, 148
income, 151–152, 158
insights, 150, 152, 158
introductions, 150–152, 158
Roll Game Film example, 139–146
of value, sequences of plays, 43
Context, defined, 168
Context for conversation:
ask for help, 117–119
authenticity vs. perfection, 168–169
congruence, 181–182, 193
convincing, 193
message matching, 167
in opening formula, xiv
play the odds, 183–193
Roll Game Film example, 171–177, 183–188
sequences of plays, xiv, 42–43
skill building, 167–177
team tone, 171–188
timing, 168–169, 189–192, 209
tone, 168–169, 180, 209
truth, 168–169, 193, 209
Conversations:
call the right play, 139–146
campaigns, 125–137, 158, 209
collaboration, 144–145, 148, 155–158, 209
content, 143, 148–153, 158, 209
context for (*See* Context for conversation)
control of, 7, 16
curiosity, 143–144, 148, 158, 209
draft/recruit prospects , 77–95
foot-in-the-door metaphor, 147–148
initial, prospects, 13–19
in opening formula, xiv

relationship rhythm establishment, 21–32
right, meaning of, 41–42
right play at right time, 33–44, 139–163
Roll Game Film example, 33–39, 139–146, 159–163
run, pass, kick, 125–137
sequences of plays, xiv, 42–44
trick plays, 159–163
"what keeps you up at night?" icebreaker, 159–163
Cooperation (*See* Collaboration)
Cost, campaign tier, 126
Creative Growth Group, 133–134, 208
Criteria for success, consequences, 69–70
Cultivate prospects, 86, 121, 209
Culture, client similarities, 62, 92
Curiosity:
in conversations, 139–146, 148, 158, 209
defined, 148
DOTS, 153–154
opening vs. manipulating, 17–18

D
Decision makers, 61, 91, 93–94
Decision making based on Opening Strategy, 73
Delivery:
client growth strategies, 88–89
platforms, 132–134
Desperation, avoiding, 19
DOTS and curiosity, 153–154
Draft/recruit prospects , 77–95

E
Education experience, 127
Engagement, moving toward, 127–128, 179–180, 201
Entertainment experience, 127–128
Enthusiasm, 19, 181
(*See also* Authenticity)
Equip for referrals/introductions, 117
Exceptions, resist managing to, 72
Executives, prioritize prospect, 93–94, 121

Existing clients as referral sources, 107
Experience as context (*See* Context for conversation)
The Experience Economy (Pine and Gilmore), 179
Experiences, campaign tiers, 126–129, 136, 158

F
Facebook, campaign delivery, 135
Favre, Brett, 191
Field position, establishing, 3–19
   avoid offensiveness, 13
   enthusiasm vs. desperation, 19
   opening:
      before closing, 16–19
      defining, 14–15
      vs. manipulating, 17–18, 200
   Roll Game Film example, 3–12
Findable, 31
Finesse for openings, xii
Florida, Richard, 57
Football metaphor (*See specific topics*)
Ford, Henry, 130
Forward toward long-term relationship, 32
Four S approach, 61–63, 91–93
Franklin, Benjamin, 119
Free:
   context of conversation, 169
   cookies as, 174–176
   relationship rhythms, 32
   sample, offering quality, 128–129
Frequency of contacts, 190–191, 193
Friendly relationship rhythm, 31–32
Front line, respect for, 97–101
Fundamentals, emphasis on, 115–116
Funding, client similarities, 62, 92

G
Game film review (*See* Roll Game Film)
Gilmore, Joe, 179
Goals, client similarities, 62, 92
Gold tier prospects, 87–88

Green, "Mean" Joe, 66
Growing Professional Services online, 208
Growth:
   client similarities, 62, 92
   prioritize prospects, 88–89

H
Hard sell, 203–205
Harvard Business Review, 64
Harvest prospects, 86, 121, 209
Heart to head, 175
Henry, Todd, 135
"How it feels to work with you?," 63, 65–67, 74
"How you do it?," 64–65, 74

I
Icebreaker "what keeps you up at night?," 159–163
Ideal client, 61–63, 89–93
Ideas exchanged, collaboration, 158
Impact of campaign, 126
Improvise, play sequence, 43–44
Income, content in conversation, 151–152, 158
Industry, client statistics, 61, 91
Information, harvest prospects, 86, 121
Insights:
   content in conversation, 150, 152, 158
   harvest prospects, 86, 121
Intent of initial conversation, 13–19
Intentional grounding, 191
Intimacy of campaign, 126
Introductions, harvest prospects, 86, 121

J
Johnson, Calvin "Megatron," 67
Jones, "Too Tall," 66
Jordan, Michael, 190
"Jordan, Joseph" (*See* Roll Game Film)

K
Kelly, Jim "Machine Gun," 67

L

Learn for referrals/introductions, 116
Levitt, Theodore, 64
LinkedIn, campaign delivery, 135–136
Location, client statistics, 61, 91
Locker room speech, 109–120
Lombardi, Vince, 115
Longevity, timing opening, 192–193

M

Maintaining openness, 197–201
Manipulating vs. opening, 17–18, 200
Mantle, Mickey, 190
Market share, client statistics, 61
"Marketing Myopia" (Levitt), 64
Matching campaign to prospects, 136
McGriff, Fred, 42
Message matching, context of conversation, 167
Model actions for referrals/introductions,
    116–117
Montana, Joe, 67

N

Networking:
    campaign delivery, 135
    collaborative community, 53–55, 58–59
    relationship rhythm establishment,
        29–32
    sequence to open relationships, 43
    social media, 93–94, 116, 134–136
    start Opening Strategy Approach, 50–52
    teamwork for , 97–108
    (*See also* Referrals and introductions)
Newsletters, campaign delivery, 135
Next meeting, reasons for, 176
Nicknames, sport, 66–67
"No" as response, 8–10, 15, 18
Nyad, Diana, 192

O

Odds of success, raising, 60
"The Open Note" coffee shop (*See* Roll
    Game Film)

Open-ends, 197–209
Opening formula, connection in, xiv
Opening Playbook online, 208
Opening plays, 3–44
    field position establishment, 1–19
    relationship establishment, 21–32
    right play at right time, 33–44
Opening Story, 70–71, 117
Opening Strategy approach:
    capabilities, 60, 63–67, 74, 209
    clients, 60–63, 74, 209
    competitors, 60, 67–68, 74, 209
    consequences, 60, 69–70, 74, 209
    defined, 59
    elements of, 47–74
    how else questions, 18
    questions to answer, xv
    Roll Game Film example, 47–55
    story form, 70–71, 73, 117
    testing, 71–73
Opening(s):
    as adjective, 14
    campaigns, 125–137, 158, 209
    as clarification, 15
    closing vs., xi, 16–19
    coda and resources, 203–209
    connections, 77–120
    context for conversation, 167–192
    conversations, 125–163
    draft/recruit prospects , 77–95
    to earn the right to close, 16–17
    field position establishment, 3–19
    first downs, 189–192
    formula for, xiv
    ideal openers, examples of, 14–15
    introductions and referrals, 109–120
    locker room speech, 109–120
    vs. manipulating, 17–18, 200
    as noun, 15
    open-ends, 197–209
    opening plays, 3–44
    opening strategy, 47–74
    play the odds, 183–193

Opening(s) (*continued*):
  preparing for, 17–18
  receivers, find fast, 109–114
  right play at right time, 139–163
  run, pass, kick, 125–137
  skill building, 167–177
  team tone, setting, 171–182
  teamwork for referrals, 97–108
  timing, 189–192
  trick plays, 159–163
  as verb, 14–15
  winning in red zone, 199–201
Open-mindedness, 207
Opponent, barriers as, xiii
Opportunities:
  anticipating, 90–91
  change as, 91
  curiosity, 154, 158
Orange tier prospects, 88

P
Pacino, Al, 115
Package your offering, 200
Payton, Walter "Sweetness," 66
Peer-to-peer round tables as delivery
    platform, 133
Perceived risk, lowering, 127
Perfection vs. authenticity, context,
    168–169
Perry, William "Refrigerator," 66
Personal benefit, 206
Peterson, Adrian, 103
Physical health benefit, 207
Pine, Joe, 179
Platforms:
  campaign tiers, 126, 129–134, 136,
      158
  delivery mechanism, 132–134
  impact and intimacy, 126
  matching to prospects, 136
  research, writing, speaking, presenting,
      130–136
  substance, 129–131

  thought leadership, 130–136
  "what if" brainstorming, 130
Play sequencing, xiv, 42–44
Play the odds, 183–188
Playbooks in sports, xii
Pocket presence, 33–39
Podcasts as delivery platform, 134–135
Premature closers, 19
Presenting programs, in campaign, 130–136
Priorities:
  connections, 86–94, 121, 209
  growth strategies, 88–89
  Opening Strategy approach to, xvi
  prospect executives, 93–94, 121
  prospect list, sequence to open
      relationships, 42
  prospect organizations, 86, 89–93
  prospects, 86–95, 121, 209
  tiers of prospects, 86–88
  time as prioritized, xvi
Proactive pursuit of prospects, 73
Productive collaboration, 155
Professional benefit, 206
Professionals as referrals source, 107
Profit benefit, 206
Programs:
  campaign tiers, 126, 130–137, 158
  impact and intimacy, 126
  matching to prospects, 136
  social media, 134–136
Prospects:
  draft/recruit, 77–95
  elite, 87
  initial conversation with, 13–19
  Opening Strategy approach, 60–63, 74,
      209
  prioritize executives, 93–94, 121
  prioritize organizations, 86, 89–93
  vs. referrals, 104–105
  relationship rhythm establishment,
      21–32
  sequence to open relationships, xiv,
      42–43

skill building, 167–177
(*See also* Clients; Referrals and
introductions; *specific topics*)
Purpose for referrals/introductions, 118

Q

Quality of prospects, 190
Questions:
capabilities, 63–67, 74
"how it feels to work with you?," 63,
65–67, 74
"how you do it?," 64–65, 74
on ideal clients, 91–92
"what if?" brainstorming, 130
"what keeps you up at night?" icebreaker,
159–163
"what you do?," 63–64, 74
"why?" and consequences, 74

R

Reagan, Ronald, 115
Receivers, find fast, 109–114
Recruit/draft prospects , 77–95
Red chip prospects, 87
Red tier prospects, 87
Red zone, 199–200
Referrals and introductions, 109–120
ask/accept help, 117–120
Ben Franklin effect, 119–120
connection, 109–120
content in conversation, 150–152, 158
emphasis on the fundamentals, 115–116
equip, 117
harvest prospects, 86, 121
learn, 116
model actions, 116–117
preferred sources of, 105–107
prequalification, 105, 108
prospects vs., 104–105
purpose for, 118
Roll Game Film example, 97–101,
109–114
sequence to open relationships, 42–44

teamwork for, 97–108
thanks and gratitude, 120
value of referral, 118–119
Reflection of strategy, 73
Reframing capabilities, 64
Regulations, client situation, 62, 93
Relationships:
authenticity in first contacts, 29–30
enthusiasm for, 19
findable, 31
forward, 32
free, 32
friendly, 31–32
inventory, cultivate prospects, 86
rhythm establishment, 21–32
Roll Game Film example, 21–27
vs. urgency for new clients, 18
(*See also* Connection)
Research programs, in campaign, 130–136
Results, campaign tier, 126
Rhythm establishment, relationships,
21–32
Right, defined, 41–42
Right experience (*See* Context for
conversation)
Right play at right time, 33–44, 139–163
play sequencing, xiv, 42–44
right, meaning of, 41–42
Roll Game Film example, 33–39,
139–146, 159–163
(*See also* Conversations)
Right relationships (*See* Connection)
Rise of the Creative Class (Florida), 57
Rockne, Knute, 115
Roll Game Film:
collaboration, 139–146
content, 139–146
context of conversation, 171–177,
183–188
conversations, 33–39, 139–146,
159–163
curiosity, 143–144
draft/recruiting prospects , 77–84

Roll Game Film (*continued*):
    maintaining openness, 197–198
    as metaphor, xiv–xv
    Opening Strategy approach, 47–55
    referrals/introductions, 109–114
    rhythm establishment, 21–27
    right plays at right time, 33–39,
        139–146, 159–163
    skill building, 171–177
    team tone, 171–177, 183–188
    teamwork for referrals, 97–101
Rose, Pete, 192
Ross, Steve, xvi
Ryan, Matt, 67

S
Sample, offering quality, 128–129
Self-praise vs. content, 149–150
Sequences of plays, xiv, 42–43
Shiny objects vs. content, 149–150
Signals, 155–157, 168
Similarities:
    clients, 61–62, 74, 92
    curiosity, 153, 158
Situational context (*See* Context for
    conversation)
Situations, clients, 62–63, 74, 93
Size of company, client statistics, 61, 91
Skill building, 167–177
"Smith, Roger" (*See* Roll Game Film)
Social media:
    to learn about prospect, 116
    programs, 134–136
    prospect executives, 93–94
Social network (*See* Networking)
Solicitation vs. content, 149–150
Sources:
    of ideal clients, 91–92
    of referrals, 105–107
Speaking programs, in campaign, 130–136
Sports metaphor, xiv–xv
    (*See also specific topics*)

Sports playbooks, xii
Statistics, clients, 61, 74, 91
Structure, client similarities, 62, 92
Substance, platforms, 129–131
Substitutes, competitors, 68, 74
Suitability, clients, 63, 74
Sun Tzu, xv, xvi
Survey initiatives as delivery platform, 133

T
Tactics, xv, xvi, 125
Tchotchkes vs. content, 149–150
Team tone:
    Roll Game Film example, 171–177,
        183–188
    setting, 171–182
Teamwork for referrals, 97–108
    benefits of, 103–104
    connection, 97–108
    ideal referral sources, 105–107
    prospects vs. referrals, 104–105
    Roll Game Film example, 97–101
Techniques for openings, xii
Testing opening, 71–73
Thanks for referrals/introductions, 120
Thought leadership, platforms, 130–136
Tiers of prospects, 86–88
Time Warner, xvi
Timing, 189–192
    accuracy, 189–190, 193
    context for conversation, 168–169,
        189–192, 209
    frequency, 190–191, 193
    longevity, 192–193
    prioritized, xvi
    in right context, 209
Tone:
    context for conversation, 168–169,
        180, 209
    team, 171–188
Touch the prospect, number to convert,
    183–188, 191

Transitions, client situation, 62, 93
Trigger points, 154, 158, 190
Triple play, 77–84
Trust:
    collaboration, 157
    referrals and introductions, 109
    vs. urgency with prospects, 18
    (*See also* Authenticity)
Truth:
    collaboration, 158
    context for conversation, 168–169,
        193, 209
    delivery, 180
    team tone, setting, 179–182

U
Unknown elements, collaboration, 156–157
Urgency for new clients, 18

V
Value:
    continuous connection with, 191
    of referrals/introductions, 118–119

W
Wabi-sabi (Japanese concept of
    imperfection), 169
"Wentworth, Sam" (*See* Roll Game Film)
"What if?" brainstorming, 130
"What keeps you up at night?" icebreaker,
    159–163
"What you do?," 63–64, 74
"Why?" and consequences, 74
Willingness to help, cultivate prospects, 86,
    121
Wish list of prospects (*See* Connection)
Writing programs, in campaign, 130–136

ABOUT THE AUTHOR

Photographer: Shannon Davis

Andrew Dietz is founder and president of Creative Growth Group, Inc., a marketing and business development firm that helps business and professional services organizations grow client relationships and revenue. Andrew is cofounder of CGG Alliance, a consortium of marketing services firms dedicated to supporting professional services organizations. He also founded the Client Advisor Awards and Summit, a national conference and awards program for professional services firms and their clients of choice.

For more information about Andrew Dietz, Creative Growth Group, and *The Opening Playbook*, visit these websites:

www.creativegrowthgroup.com

www.growingprofessionalservices.com

www.clientadvisorawards.com

www.openingplaybook.com

You also may enjoy Andrew's previous book, *The Last Folk Hero: A True Story of Race and Art, Power and Profit.*